Hatching the Ideal

Beliefs

IHSAN JONES

ISBN:978-0-578-75845-9

DEDICATION

Dedicated to my children and grandchildren. Especially those who gave words of support and encouragement at times when most needed.

CONTENTS

1	**Not Seeing Things as I Want to See it**	Pg. 3
2	**On the Doorstep of Change**	Pg. 18
3	**Life's Calling US**	Pg. 34
	PART TWO	
4	**My Very Own Dictionary**	Pg. 43
5	**What is happening during The Exchange?**	Pg. 50
6	**Technific!**	Pg. 70
7	**NEVERMIND**	Pg. 86
8	**Earths Linkages are known by design**	Pg. 111
9	**Road Map**	Pg. 137
10	**Graduation**	Pg. 149

I'm not a writer

I'm an experiencer

And there's a difference.

Experiencers get to relate what took place.

There can be a different experience for everyone thereby resulting in many stories.

The difference between a writer and an experience, is that

People that tell stories will add- in their additions. An Experiencer usually doesn't- they tell it like it is.

I see differently- as felt through an Experiencer

IJ

1 NOT SEEING THINGS AS I WANT TO SEE IT

I can't believe this is happening. Its starting all over again, and it tends to happen out of the blue. Nothing prompts this, and it tends to come in succession.

I could be held in suspended animation (at bey) until the event is over. Other times I could be participating. There is a pattern, and I've come to know it well.

The dreams I have are never encouraged. Who would look forward to experiencing something that is unpleasant? I certainly don't! And I suspect that no one else would, either. The cost of having dreams is to pay its toll. The toll of which, is uncertain. I played out the events that were drumming in my head like I was covering the nightshift.

It was dark, and I was familiar with the surroundings.

Across the street (directly across from my house), something was amiss. I couldn't quite make it out at first, but it seemed that my son (second son) was somehow involved. I stared at the figures and what I witnessed was disturbing. My son, (for some unknown reason) was into it (having a rough time) with some unsavory fellows. Those fellows, it seemed, wanted to "do him in". I heard it loud and clear coming from the dude that was standing across the street. He elicited others to do his dirty work. Although he may have gotten in a few punches himself, he left it up to his lieutenants (those that listened- to him) to do his dirty work.

I felt nauseated and even a bit scared. I knew that I couldn't (really) intervene, but I had to. I walked across the street in a huff after seeing my son being made to kneel as if his life meant nothing because it was readily apparent that he couldn't fight back. Don't get me wrong, my son is a fighter, and I knew what he was capable of…when he was sober. He definitely would want to stand up to the likes of this kind. My son (not being squeamish) kneeling…meant that he was subdued. He was surrounded by at least four individuals and knew that he couldn't escape.

This was the dream I had, and for a mother that type of dream could be daunting.

I knew little about the situation. Didn't even know why it had happened. That's how dreams are I suppose. You could be thinking one way, and it end up as another.

The mood had changed, the scene had switched, and somehow, I was thrust into it.

I yelled out loud at the top of my voice, although it was nighttime and too dark, to actually, see someone.

I heard the voice coming through loud acting as if it didn't have a care in the world for anyone intervening.

I ran across with my greatest "bluff", in hopes that he could escape. As a mother when we hear these things...having threats to our sons, the battle cry would be turned on!

The guy looked at me as I tried to save my son-after hearing him say "just go ahead and kill him' in an unkind voice that was nonchalant.

I ran with the gusto of a person acting as if I had a weapon, knowing actually, that I didn't.

I tried to scream out to my son, telling him to get up and to run. But his head hung low the entire time and my only interaction with him was this lone voice.

I hated that something like this could happen. Especially, to my son.

"I have a weapon! I yelled. Bold enough to stare at the other person as I was crossing the street giving me the strength to say something. Although I didn't say what type it was. I wanted him to assume it was a gun. You gotta bring a gun to a gun fight-so I'm told. But this was a fist fight; and not any weapon would do. Especially when you're out numbered.

I walked briskly in a stride at a hurried pace approaching the situation...the guy didn't even lift his head even as I was talking. Nor did my son. To the people surrounding him, this didn't matter. It was as if I never mattered in this brief encounter even if I was brave and wanting to help. Then the dream ended.

The dream ended as if cut off from its conclusion; only felt it. Right before the dream ended, I felt the plotting and planning that had been done from these folks that were surrounding my son. It seemed that everything, as part of the conclusion- would NOT, be OK.

I called my oldest son, his older brother, almost immediately after the dream. I related to him the story of what had taken place and told him it was something that I felt deeply. Deeply enough to call him and relate the story.

"Is everything Ok, I said to him, frantically. You gotta' find your brother! Make sure that he's ok because I just had a dream. The dream was so powerful that it felt real and that's why I'm feeling the need to have to call you- to have you check up on him."

He listened and then replied, OK. He assured me that he would follow up or at least check on his brother's whereabouts.

Then I called my oldest daughter.

"Mom. What you said sounds exactly like what has happened to him before. Remember, when he got jumped and beat up?

I had to acknowledge that she was telling the truth. Yes, I answered.

I asked myself, Why, was I having this dream now? Was it dejavue, or could this really be happening to him again?

"You never know, I told her. Let's just hope that he is safe."

Because of that, I had to tell her that my dreams don't always have to be about the person. Usually, there will be somebody else. Someone with similarities characteristics, and the likeness.

I left it at that. Worried still...and wishing my dream had never happened.

When my dreams are intense like that and give detail, I tend to worry. I take a precaution by telling someone. Not that they could do anything, but in my son's case if we had found him maybe we could prevent it by warning him ahead of time to be more careful because his lifestyle could be catching up to him. This seemed to be the biggest worry.

A couple of weeks had passed and in the interim I had talked to my son. He called me so I felt somewhat relieved but not quite. Sometime later, we got reported the news of something like this happening to someone that was very close-to all of us. This person was like my very own family.

The closeness or likeness of the person could be related and the problem with having dreams like this, is that you could never know...what could be the outcome. And no matter how hard it is to have experienced this, right after, or closely thereafter, the dream, it seems, will pan out. So, I am not necessarily caught off guard. But trapped in a cycle. A cycle of which, unfortunately, the dreams themselves, will tell me that they're true.

I cried, of course. Just like I was upset through most of my dream. That angst I felt, had come back. This clearly was a person that was expressly represented in that dream.

It's because I need a release. I need to feel some type of comfort in my hopes and my prayers that these types of dreams (the ones that I tend to have from time to time) will not and cannot be true!

I never have a sense of ownership, but I do feel that I'm vested.

The reason I have a 'vested interest', is because I care. I can care so deeply that I would have to relive the pain. And the worse part, is knowing that these dreams could never be over unless, and until...something really happens.

I've always knew that I was a 'sponge' in a life- line succession of having experiences of this type that could be connected to events.

It's a cycle. And it's unfortunate that I have to bear the 'brunt' of feeling the agonizing pain of any dreams that I could be having, aftermath; knowing full well that I could never prevent it. If it was going to happen. It was going to happen anyway, whether, I had dreamed it or not.

The aftermath, of seeing those things wasn't the conclusion, but just the start of how it would affect my life. The impact of knowing- is mostly devasting. And- also knowing that it all had seemed to be linked to a bit- of clairvoyance.

Who doesn't ever want to 'go back' to a dream and reverse its circumstances? I did, and most definitely would...if I could. You can tell by my interactions within that particular; dream that I already had brought a 'knife' or maybe even a gun to what was a fist fight with the intention of scaring off the predators.

My son would have been released from any harm if my actions had panned out. But the dream ended abruptly, and I didn't know it's outcome, whether my son could be saved or not. I somehow felt the opposite. If those folks in the dream had not taken any further action, the dream I felt, might have been different.

I'm getting old, and I'm tired.

The dreams I feel, have been going on too long. Throughout my life I've had this experience. The experience of "seeing things ahead" as they call it. Whether or not it's dreams, there can always be something that's left in my heart-which is a void.

I never asked for any of this.

And in my heart of all hearts...I'd rather dispense with it completely.

And that's the truth!

Clarivoyance

Clarivoyance, is just a word. But it can be seen as gleaning through episodes.

There are many episodes in our lives that we tend to ignore, or maybe that are so profound that we can never forget.

When we have been gifted with insight there is a presence. We are given hindsight and foresight, put together, and oddly enough, that is supposed to be considered a blessing.

Sometimes the 'knowing' of too much, or too little doesn't matter. It is the 'before' and 'after' that counts most.

This book is about those blessings that I have received through my very own foresight and they include my visions. Visons of which, are similar, to my dreams when I have them, and that I have no control over.

I can never predict the outcome or circumstances of any event before it is happening. It will only be that I have 'seen' it.

Flashbacks

I'm not a writer-one who tells stories.

I'm an experiencer-and there's a difference.

Experiencers, get to relate to you, what took place.

There can be a different experience for everyone. Which means telling a different story.

People that tell stories will add in their additions.

Experiencers are often tied to clairvoyance and premonitions.
Premonitions that develop later, into insight.

My experiences started a long time ago. When I was a little girl.

I could be having flashbacks or dejavue moments about what it meant to be a little girl in a large family.

I come from a large clan of siblings. There were nine of us. My parents were as attentive as most parents I suppose since they had to keep up with us.

What I noticed from a very, early age, about myself that was unique, was that I tended to be a 'soulwatcher'. A soulwatcher is someone who could be having premonitions early on but didn't know it. It would take having the flashbacks later, on for anything to emerge.

As a soulwatcher I was tied to the bloodstream- and I can't help but think that I may have been in a long line of succession and that somehow, now it's connected to me. It may be my heritage that was passed down to me.

Soulwatchers, can be different, I suppose for everyone. For me, it was my deepest connections. And I do know that I have felt it through my blood.

Blood ties form our deepest connections and they can be closely guarded. Since they can be held as family 'secrets', we might not always know who our next of kin is. There is some strangeness to what occurs with the blood. If somehow, we are related, we won't necessarily be joined. Bloodstreams are occurring everywhere and with them comes a sense of belonging.

The configuration of families is not the issue. But the closeness of ties...is.

You can feel it sometimes when something is amiss and happening with your family. I know, I could.

I was always more sensitive to the fighting and arguing.

As a little girl, I'd see things different than most-I suppose. I'd want to run and hide or put my head beneath a pillow. I suppose that part is normal, but me, wanting to run away became a central theme.

I thought somehow that I could stop or prevent everyone from fighting. And from a little girl's perspective, this would be a daunting task. I was deeply affected and moved by being unsettled in the moment. The flashbacks I remember, were mostly of me running away.

I ran away hoping someone would notice and that I could get them to stop. I wanted to 'pause' whatever was going on just for a moment to say, "hey, look at me...don't you see how this is affecting me? I'm crying (on the inside) just look." But no one seemed to care. I never could stop the fighting, even by my running away.

That's also how I dealt with things later on. Especially if there was a crisis. Leaving the scene (of the potential) crime would be my greatest form of refuge which became my escape. But I also knew that leaving didn't disconnect me. It just meant that I had wanted to fastforward the situation and make it go away. So, I am not surprised to find at all, that the blood was the catalyst. The streaming of blood that's flowing through my veins meant that I felt-Everything!

I used to run and hide while screaming loudly at the top of my lungs for folks to stop-this was how I knew that whatever it is that goes on in my family-I could never escape.

These deep ties were the catalyst for me coming into my visions. And although they would happen much later, I feel that this is when it started. It was when I was a little girl. I am a soul watcher for my family and a deep streamer of subconscious connections that can afford me previsions before and after the fact of anything ever happening that's a result of discord.

People want to say that 'we're tapped' into a higher conscious and awareness; I don't want to call it that. Although there are progressive thoughts that can lead us to …somewhere. We don't necessarily know where that direction is. All we can do is 'feel' our way through whatever is happening, and later on try to gain some perspective. For me, personally, I felt that my connection, was the bloodstream. I don't feel that my soul watching has any other purpose except to stream the consciousness of which I am already aware. And it is from those that I receive it directly, that I have an intimate connection (the people I dream about). My perspectives are coming from that. Self- imposed and self- inflicted pain…I never reacted to any of it. I was more passionate about the way in which I felt things; the meaning of which meant that I wanted the best for everyone. And that if the situation couldn't be resolved by say…my fifth, grade antics…then I could distance myself and run far, far away. The irony of being placed (in the family) as a soul watcher, is that no matter how far you run…you still can be -deeply, connected.

My Quote: "I'm a Soul Watcher because, if I'm not seeing the actual 'people', then I must be watching their Souls- and it's been through the dreams" IJ

2 ON THE DOORSTEP OF CHANGE

I've graduated through stages. I've gone through what's called iterations. It felt as though each iteration has been life changing.

So, I am taken through events that will eventually catch up.

Too often we tell our stories from hindsight, which is rearview. Many of us have been unable to see through any of our clandestine adventures, we'd often prefer to have peered through the glass.

Peering through glass whether light or dark shouldn't matter. It's inevitable that no matter what we see...if it's going to appear...will show up.

That's why we take different paths. That is also why our experiences are not the same.

The doorstep to change is standing right beneath our feet. It's not necessarily high up in the clouds. Yes, the clearing of the sky can represent the clouds moving and shifting the fogginess from our minds), but the sky, is not the destination.

Doorsteps can be unseen. And not realized until you've actually been taken to the very destination. As floating mirrors, oftentimes we can never see the stairsteps. The clouds; will go away. Our very own, memorabilia, hangs as remnants from the discoveries from our past. Both past, present and future must collide and serve as soundchecks in order for us to get our visions. Presently, we are on the ground. In the future we might be flying high peering through mirrors in the looking glass. Isn't that the way we think?

That something, somewhere could be watching...our every action?

We see things through structures. Structures that have been built high enough to reach the clouds, but are they inroads into heaven?

There are a lot of the ways to think about our connections. My blood line connection is one. I don't try to reach the sky to solve my problems but I do look in heavens direction.

It is an inward compass, and we all can reach it. Flying high above to reach something else, is not the answer. The answer can be right here staring you in the face. Probably, when walking the grounds of discovery you will have to take alternate routes.

That is what I've always wanted to do in life. Make the problems go away. We all do, I suppose...to some extent.

Discovering the structures of what the mirrors show is very, different from discovering heaven. But it all can be tied and wrapped up to our discord. We may want to look for something different that's not coming from us, but it is not the mirrors, but the mirrors reflectors, that will expose the truth. You can look at the skies all you want. But heaven will be very different when you get there. The mirrors are a side show, and no matter what we tend to go through- they are reflectors. Mirrors can expose the truth about everything- no matter what one imagines. Mirrors give rising and can reflect off of the sun to reveal everything.

Life is a holding cell and no matter what we do, it has been built into the structure.

The Structure of Life Brings Changes

I didn't know that there were iterations when I wrote my first book. After writing it however, I did wonder what was next. It would be going through those iterations (of development) and my writing the next series of books, that my visions would manifest. Each book represented a stage. A stage that I now see as being a part of my evolution.

You'd have to wonder what next, right? Even if you're doing something that wasn' t planned; you'd likely have to peer as if looking into the future through a glass. So, iterations don't just happen. They're thrust upon us when we least expect it. That's the way it has happened for me.

It was the ringing of the door bell that would represent my next stop of what I would call an iteration. I'd had plenty of clarivoyant moments. But this one was succinct.

I heard the door bell ringing loud and clear and I arose to answer it. I had been sleeping soundly, undisturbed. When I woke up, no one there. I didn't go downstairs to actually answer the door I was just startled from my sleep. The ringing was like a loud ding dong and then you could hear silence. I knew that sound was familiar but couldn't put my hands on it. I discovered it later that it was a very, familiar doorbell sound one that we all could recognize. Whatever had wanted to wake me from my sleep, had done its job.

Then there was the loud knocking on the door as if someone was beating desperately. I could hear the banging in the distance but instead I woke. It wasn't a dream I had figured out, because those sounds were distinct. Someone, or something, coming from somewhere had wanted to wake me up! But, no one was actually there. It happened more than once. And over the course of a week I'd say, and there was time, it seemed, like days that were in between the doorbell rings and the knocks.

Who it was? I don't know. Someone that didn't want me to fall asleep to hard I suppose because I was having health problem. These flashbacks from my memories will never let me forget the sound effects.

I consider it to be original for something to wake you up this way. Something that you know, can feel in your heart is not really isn't there.

Sleeping beauty had arose only to be kept safe. It was because something wanted to keep me safe.

It definitely- was not because someone was teasing me.

Sometimes we don't find out what's sensible about our dreams until way later. But usually it is in those flashing moments that we sometimes can tell.

I had to really think long and hard about Who it was and what it meant.

For some reason I had been sleeping soundly likely snoring from not only being tired but from having been kept awake, due to my inability to sleep the previous nights. My mind was adrift from the caffeine and I had been having heart palpations. Nothing I did that week, could help me fall asleep any faster either, like listening to sleep sounds and soft waves on my cell phone. The sleep app that I tried intermittently, wasn't working. So, once I finally did pass out, I slept hard.

So, it was something I felt, that had a duty to wake me.

When I finally realized what the knocking and the doorbell ringing was for, I was relieved. Because if it had of been for something else-like teasing me, that would have been too hard to fathom. Eventually, I was back to my normal sleeping habits and haven't heard the door knocking.

Yes, we can be taken back to heaven – but sometimes I think it is heaven knocking on our door- or perhaps, ringing a doorbell.

As an Experiencer, all I wanted to do was relate my stories.

That's how I approach things now. And it's because of having already written several books. The dreams were acting as the holding cell that lead to the foundation. But the dreams themselves were not the destiny.

Understanding them was.

Clearly, by now, Divine wisdom had struck. And it was the stroke of the pen /keyboard, is how those strokes were felt.

It was another iteration- this time, but one that was Divine.

I call them previsions now because they weren't exactly, the full thing.

Nine Steps

There were nine steps to my iterations. I'll be explaining them later. This is book number 9. In the following chapters I will also be Connecting the dots.

* This book contains a dictionary, a Pictionary, and my thoughts that are free flowing from divine captivity.

Foundations

Foundations are the embodiment of our living truths.

What we have is called fortune and misfortune.

Guidance, and no guidance.

We can't walk in our truths until we've been led astray. We cannot properly, balance something to reset it unless we are capable of insight.

If we haven't missed out on anything, then we can't ever know.

Knowledge has these foundations. And these are the embodiments of our ever- living truths that's coming from our foundations. We miss somethings and we get others, but we cannot have it all.

It all relies on a spectrum. The spectrum of growth that's coming from our spirit. Our spirit and will to maintain life.

We can grow by faith and in leaps and bounds but we can never destroy what the foundation has laid.

Foundations are our fortunes. But they are also missed opportunities.

They are fortunes that we can realize in our hearts.

A full and rich spectrum will give you more fortunes and less- missed opportunities considered as advancements. Foundations are set as enhancements for our- lifecycles.

As we take any 'new' steps forward-we can claim them.

Fortune is the hearts and minds of those who can say - I've lived.

We're fortunate when we can look back upon the foundations. Springing from these foundations, nothing sustains us better than knowing that we can grow. So, as we're sprinkled with success; here and there, it won't be that way for everybody.

Spectrums can be different for everyone. But they are coming from, and belong to, the same foundation.

We have to be a part of- a foundation. It is a requirement for living.

We can't go on, move forward, and or continue, unless we can also look back. Foundations, begin us, but retrospect is the interim of all of our passages. To move forward and past anything that's sprung from its foundation, there will be limits on looking back. These are iterations. Iterations that can increase and mold our understanding of what was designed for us to build from.

The Mold

It Only happens if You See it

Substance isn't guaranteed a life. Only to exist.

There is no way to see every substance thats floating in the air or laying on the ground.

There is this thing called existence, and it only happens once.

It happens in a moment of instantaneous combustion, or it freezes with time and seeps its way onto something...anything.

And since life can't exist on its own, we have to do our part to make it happen.

In the bigger picture, there's this thing called substance that happens to be 'life' if you see it or feel its aura.

To exist, means that something is there. And there- could actually be anywhere.

To be alive is to acknowledge and recognize the presence of substance.

Substance is instantaneous, meaning that it happens through combustion. But substance also could be considered an 'instance'.

It is an instantaneous combustion and evolution of material.

The thing about substance is that it didn't just come out of nowhere. It had to be made.

So, being 'made' is what we call being 'chosen' to have a 'instance' of a life.

*Our bodies have been given a life and chosen to live in a sustainable pattern. That is the mold.

Life on its own doesn't guarantee existence. It grants you the Extenuation of what's already there.

Substance in its purest form is formulated as absence. When something isn't there it is considered gone. So, that would be the first step to making the formula. A formula can be anything that's usable for combustion. This life erupts out of nowhere based on the blueprint of its preexisting pattern. Which includes absence. Absence appears as gaseous without odor or fumes. Most gaseous substance will have an odor and that is how it can be identified.

First, you have to see it.

But you can only tell that it's a gas by its fumes.

The odor or presence of a substance doesn't need our acknowledgement.

Life exists on its own (which originally would be in a gaseous state) and is extracted from a bubble which is its shell.

If first, you should have to see it, to acknowledge its presence, that would be our first introduction into our awareness of everything that has what's called--presence.

Seeing is believing, as the saying goes, however, not knowing about something doesn't make it any less real.

Something has to be 'made' for it to be considered as substance. The extraction of substance isn't rare because we can see it coming from our bodies. So does the spawning process- that gives us our extensions.

Each 'instance' of birth is initially how we are introduced. It is how we came into the world to exist side by side with other creatures. Being born-or spawning, guarantees that life extends itself through infusion and transformation which is the substance being developed and formed. An instance of birth gives us the formation to exist as a life. The form that exists is coming from its preexisting blueprint.

We live through what's called an iteration. It is an iteration of life flowing through passageways. The iteration has an interaction or start but it also has a button whereby it could be pushed to keep us alive or turned on.

Coming from out of 'nowhere' is to be developed. The development of substance has its linkage to 'unknown'. What's unknown is linked to divinity. Our rhythmic response to what is unknown occurs in cycles. And it's through these cycles that we get to acknowledge the 'planning' of the substance.

Since the blueprint of our substance already exists. And it is that we can be made in an instance-an instance of our very own combustion that's self- made; we can be extended what's called-a life.

So, life is a series of our fluctuations through these pre-existing patterns that's generated from the flow of what can be seen and unseen.

A gaseous state is required- as a way of seeping through the cavities.

The cavities can be literally, the connecting points (similar to- rivers) that exist between us.

Holding Cell

You could be a holding cell for a blueprint, or, you could already be in your gaseous state. A holding cell is a frame, or form.

A form is also the formula for the preexisting blueprint that was developed through extraction.

Life is extended as a courtesy of the life's form (as a figure) being able to flow (as in rivers) or join with -every other situation, particularly with other instances that was created.

So, an 'instance' becomes a generation of substance as it can co-exist in the reality of everything else.

We must 'see it', to 'believe' it, otherwise we exist in our gaseous state which means we're not there.

The 'common' courtesy of being extended a life form- is to demonstrate the efficiency and expediency of creating an 'instance'.

All cycles are extensions of a common factor called development.

The choice we make (within our circumstances) are all connected to the cycles of fluctuation.

It is the 'rivers' in our bodies that give us the common factors. The blood vessels and veins can be connected to common things like eyes, ears, nose, etc.

Seeing, hearing and smelling draws from the aura of our surroundings.

The common courtesy of the extension of the neospasm is to let us know that we are spawns.

3 LIFE'S CALLING US

Neospasms

Neospasms were creating the spawns to reflect the images of themselves as a means of their own projection to counterbalance the effects of (themselves) having to duplicate.

That image is taken and coming from a reposed position. Tucked from under a wing with shoots and sprouts.

So, are we plants?

Yes, and no, is the simple answer.

What we can say is that we are trans(planted), and that our transitory spirit is the most important part of us ever being made.

Recoiling; means changing positions. And for the neospasms to change-as in an outgrowth-its pre patterns must already be set.

Neospasms can be as fuzzy, bare, jelly, or any other substance that can hold its weight. That is the recoiling and repositioning. And since neospasms are an original blueprint, any substance, that's formed, can find and make its way.

Substance has its ability to reposition-that is the recoiling. But it is all coming from the foundation. The foundation which is the fountain of youth from which everything has sprung or springs forward.

Spawns

Spawning creates the natural balance of our daily lives. To exist, is to manifest. Spawns are derivatives of their own nature.

Once a new spawn exists, the old (or pre-existing spawn) repositions around it and everything it does revolves around the spawns, new growth.

It's like a mother and father protecting its youth.

We can no longer be a singular once we exist. We, too, must carry a spawn.

But the spawn isn't what you think. The spawn appears as a baby but also gets to be the master. Not the master as a blueprint, But the master of its own destiny. We are the masters of our own destiny and as spawns, we continue to be the outgrowths of neospasms.

Everything exists is an order. We cannot upset the order in any way, shape, or fashion.

What does it mean to Be Connected to Divinity?

The connection with divinity is coming from the spasm. The spasm, as a blueprint, has originated from a master design. The neospasm is the blueprint of everything that we're connected to that was existing before us. A neospam gives us our heart, our brain. Its master- design and look, is what we come from. A linkage to this bond is undeniable, but spasms haven't reached their 'everlasting' state. They exist, through divinity.

Blueprints of neospasms are extracted and created to formulate as 'new' instances' of substance (by Divinity). So, the spasm becomes 'new' again and never gets old because of the ability to offshoot as a spawn.

The creation of a 'magical' combustion didn't happen on its own. It was created through the spirits of (Godly-like) creatures.

Foreign or alien- there is substance that can be seen and that has been generated through the patterns.

And it is real and true because it exists. We exist in an 'instance' of Divinity combining its substance with the patterns.

God(ly) -like creature (those that invent) are known to have created neospasms, and they can give them to various modes of living space (cosmos). *divine wisdom*

If we, as humans, want to place one particular substance at the helm and call it God-so be it.

But there seems to be more than one existing pattern.

For us, it shouldn't matter, since we return to our own as natural configuration.

We can only be reconfigured again, after its regeneration. Or the regeneration, of an instance. Which is to create.

Our continuation has fluctuation. There will be fluctuation in the rivers flowing.

However, what's key to life, is the existence of the form.

This isn't novel- this is a fact. And it can be seen in life's patterns.

We can't criss-cross the wires when we have been chosen to operate under the neospasms preexisting blueprint.

If there are any 'new' discoveries of preexisting forms that are made- I think we can see them. But I don't think there will be any new substance arriving here soon. And some have already become extinct, we have discovered (like the dinosaurs), or have transitioned their substance through recoiling that was necessary to evolve as other creatures, i.e; large lizards have become smaller due to exchanging their bodies formation to adapt to environmental conditioning etc. there are other examples and reasons given for forms and figures swapping as in switching out their life cycles to reconfigure, but the original blueprint from which they can be matched-remains intact. So, nothing new, has originated, as, of yet. There have been no new body formations as coming from the original designs. Divinity hasn't 'chosen' to select any other body forms as originations (blueprints), other than what we have already seen or come to know.

To be connected to Divinity means that we have a free- flowing substance that's transitory that was deposited in our bodies. It's an instance where life can appear as free flowing (not attached), however it is still coming off of a pattern. The free-flowing nature of our substance was made to coincide with any of the patterns (of the holding cells) of life.

Anything that has been struck from the master blueprint, divinity has touched it first. Thus, divinity can have a direct connection with us (as spawns) even bypassing the neospasm.

The inertia that's built into the pattern combines and connects our spirit with divinity. Inertia is also what creates the pattern of combustion and forces the materials to combine. Inertia is the movement of generation. Generation, and regeneration, is the 'grace' that divinity provides us. The tediousness of the task of our making, also meant extending the blueprint of the neospasms; and so 'grace' was extended as well, so that spawns didn't have to carry the heavy burden alone. We could also have intervention from divinity if, and when, a neospasm no longer required our services. *(By spawning, we lend them our services).

We can see ourselves as having 'figures' that are in between us, and our original maker. In the chain and order of things, neospams should have to keep watch over us because we come directly from them. Each neospasm pattern, whether it is a creature known to us or not, is coming from its original blueprint. How else, could we, as spawns keep regenerating. The cells of the neospasms are lent 'tissue' interjected as new species into the podcast of an abode aka -mode of living-initially. Then, our calling card with divinity is held as a 'trump' card so that no souls can ever be lost.

We are made because we were extracted from neospasms as offshoots of their original blueprint.

Neospasms are the designs of what God-like creatures -have made.

As imprints, or spawns of continuation, we get to do something that's rare and unique. We also get to go back into that from which we came. We've always known there has been something between us and divinity. But with divinity-there is also, a direct line of communication that surpasses any of its designs.

***Joining- or Splitting and pairing of Cells**

The two entities had to be joined- together again, there couldn't be, just one (male and female).

Much of it had to do with our bodies built- in attraction mechanism. So, two cells that previously had one form, split. (it was built as one initially from extraction). And from that one, came many.

The neospasms wasn't split, as in a break- up. The split was to get us to recognize where our development was coming from. As a rubber band, effect, splitting afforded us more opportunities. Double personalities could resist-but also preserve the circuitry wiring of the entire species as a means of protection. Joining- was essential to understand spawning because spawns undergo the changes of making two halves that are split- then rejoin them, to make a whole other.

Spawns can be seduced-to be rejoined.

4 MY VERY OWN DICTIONARY

Dictionary (as seen through my lens)

Purpose- -to find it

-to have already known it

-to realize the beauty and obstacle at the same time

On Purpose -if you did it intentionally, you know

Of Purpose -to realize it, where it can come into actualization

-to seek, to find, to do…purpose could be any of these

*I think that once we have discovered it (what our purpose is), then it takes on meaning and becomes purposeful. Which means…you are 'full of purpose'.

Causation- -The cause of things; how they come about

Actualization- -The realness of something having shape or form even if it's words or deeds.

*an actual cause of something coming into realization

Realization- -a tangible substance that could be developed (born) in an instance once it's known about-which is discovery of an actual cause.

Prototype- -to synthesize the 'awareness' of all of the above

*similar to photosynthesis where realizing that anything could be possible based on what's real.

A form-becomes a prototype.

Neospasms are not 'causation'; but they can cause substance to be formed, reformed and reshaped because of the split.

The splitting of cells starts initially with the first formation.

Two entities split-that's the first. Shapes and forms then represent the (newest) development of any formation.

All formations have a history. The history is tied to the mannerism in which the shape is formed.

The ignition of life is not the spinning of substance. Life is revved up through cataclysmic efforts from the volume of pressure. The pressure of things forming together makes a substance.

There is an instance-that substance can be made from the excitement of which results in a flash.

We can't see it...the trigger. But it's there.

It's felt. That's the connection, the feeling of the moment can't be contained unless it's preconceived. Preconception means that the substance that's forming, has to live through a flash-the flash that creates the substance.

At the minutest level- that instance represents life and the life forms through the causation of movement that's coming from substance.

There's one more thing to do, which is pull the lever. A lever represents leveling of substance. Once the substance is forming a shell has been created from the flash. The flash was the 'sealing' of substance that was created in an instance. Real substance can only live if there is something to contain it. That's the way it takes on its shape and form.

Initiation-

The initiation of substance was oral. Most things that are spoken; actually, can come into existence. It was narrated by a figure (of being) called Supreme Entity that lives among us.

This supreme duality of a form created an instance. An instance of causation in which several forms were developed.

If it were not for the various forms of substance being able to gel (or liquidate)-to form into something else...we wouldn't have an actual life.

Iteration-

There are iterations to the forms. Each form of substance is to relive and recharge its life-again, as if having a battery.

The iteration of a substance's life (cycle) is as movement. Even (free standing), the substance that's contained, must move again to begin to agitate and develop on its own.

That's the cycle-it is the iteration.

You can plainly see that an iteration means-to seek its own. It means that anything that tends to develop, works in a pattern. Patterns can tell the substance which 'instance' of causation it has experienced so it can live. It's like an invitation.

Patterns-

So, the patterns become formed as linear, divergent, and digressive levers that begin as circular but end as continuous.

A shell- which is a containment, is closed. The divergent nature of a shell is to be closed-forever, however, its digression can move among the linear scale to become outreached. The pulling of substance is to retain its pressure/volume.

New forms--outstretched

New substance--more created instances

What gets Agitated?

Agitation- Agitation is the continuous pressure to move the substance.

That's what our spasms (of life) do. They create new instances by pulling the volume away from its origination.

If there is an instance of a substance being made as 'see through', does that mean it isn't there?

The answer is No. Because it means that there is absence.

Is color required to identify the 'absence' of the parameters and properties that are present in the substance?

No. Only the realization that the substance has had an instance to occur- is required.

Patterns show the real substance of what they are. So, if you ever want to see proof that there's a pattern, you should have to look for what the pattern shows.

For example- if a substance is 'outstretched'. It contains the riddles of an equation. Each pattern is formed of advanced materials for substance to create its greatest movement or agitation.

Each movement of an instance that's created, will 'show up' the pattern of its substance. Whether circular, linear, motionless...created sensors need to become activated. This is done inversely, to offset any mistakes.

Therefore, whatever is done in reverse (such as standing on one's head) substitutes the directional flow of the pattern. Which will affect it from creating movement on its own. It becomes 'stuck, in gear while it is returning to its original state. The state agitates to resolve the missed activation.

5 WHAT IS HAPPENING DURING THE EXCHANGE?

The Exchange happens once- and then we are regenerated (if we have been turned off).

It doesn't matter if the body knows or doesn't know about this exchange because there are signals.

The signals are the 'switches' whereby we are able to turn 'off' and 'on'.

The behavior is the pattern. Patterns that have been built into the code.

Code 'switching' is not new. We have been doing this for generations, even before we became new spawns.

Spawns are the parts of the code that form the 'makeup' of our bodies. It is separated from when we are 'code switched' through transition.

We have direct linkages to recover and to be recalled.

An extended souls code switching is through the linkage of their lineage and heritage. So, it would be similar to DNA but not quite. There is a 'root' that connects the direct line to divinity. If code switching continues, we will be considered as everlasting. We are not the antiques of our past. We are always formulated as new even if we seem as preexisting. What's ancient about us is the forms of development. They haven't changed. Only the neospasm is in the ultimate form of exclusive substance' that can exist on its own. That is because it is the original form.

Our patterns are the extensions that are coming from off the patterns of alien beings. Most likely, we have chosen to call them that because they appear to live outside of us. They want us separate however, so they (as in we) can keep adding and making us through extensions.

We are extensions of the plasma of cosmic forces that are in our genes and coming from the new code driven by our 'likeness' (heritage and lineage), that gets passed through the cells.

For each pattern that exists within a cell- it becomes exclusive.

What we have uncovered, thus far, is a bridge to our switching. A switching mechanism that's being 'controlled' by what's outside of the body. A spirit of foreign body that exists and is considered to be as an alien source.

We are always becoming the 'new spawns' because we are their extensions. Spawns that are born as new babies.

The alien spirit- from which we are extracted- uses the bodies configuration to control it. There is a root cause to everything and it's because we're coded via our lineage and heritage.

The other root cause, that's spiritual, has been done to plan an escape route.

The petri dish that holds us – I call it a petri dish but its really our earthly compound. A petri dish means you're held under some kind of condition, and for us, that is both metaphysical and physical.

But the petri dish can't always hold us. We can escape our encapsulation by forming into gases.

Gases are spiritual surroundings of inoculant substance that can be considered as incubation.

So, as we go through the exchange (of the incubation of life), our bodies form has already planned its means of escape. We escape by submission to the signals.

An Experience I once had was through something I call- Observation… I had witnessed a woman's body (in figure and form) being transported, as if floating through air. She was in her complete body form (meaning no alterations) and she was fully clothed. There was free space that existed around her as an aura- but since I was there too, sharing the space- I couldn't tell initially, what it was about. How could someone float through air on their own? She was free-flowing but was guided. It appeared that her spirit had left her. In retrospect, I would come to recognize that her code switching- meant she must have been turned off.

The lady's linkage to the patterns must have been coming through as signals because she was incapable of ascertaining her surroundings.

This was all via my observance. As I had been taken to this place myself.

My observance was being done auspiciously. And it was capricious that I could even be seeing this. I was in the exact same sphere as this 'floating lady', however, I hadn't realized the depth and magnitude of what it all meant. And especially what it meant to be 'taken'. That was something that I witnessed.

I now have concrete proof that it was the aliens that were controlling her. Although they looked a lot like us-as humans in some ways and mannerisms, I couldn't see them completely so I couldn't tell.

We exist through aliens that provide the linkage to our discovery – but these aliens (well, divinity) has also devised (for us) an escape plan.

I don't think that we're totally trapped within our distinct biosphere either. I think we can leave it. Even if we're subjects, we're constantly being introduced as body substance through a string of code. So, it would not matter necessarily which species can be transferred.

Any neospasm can be moved forward (because of its outward shell nature) to be present as a part of reconfiguration. Why bother making something similar; if we're all the same? Because similar species, can co-exist.

I don't expect (as I go through the exchange) to be greeted by...let's say...an alligator. Because that would be another form. But it would not be impossible as far as I'm concerned. Why else would they, as our makers, conceal their bodies original form? Most likely, we can be "taken' by exposure to and from something we already know. The petri dish (as our habitat containment) is an induction. It is how we have been introduced. The reasons connected to that introduction (of the neospasm) into this hemisphere- is beyond our understanding. All we can really know, is that when we are called-we must go back.

We exist through iterations. Iterations of learning to control our behavior -that's held within the petri dish.

These iterations can be known as spiritual adaptation of substance. Because the substance is aware that it is in the petri dish. And it must become as gaseous, to escape.

Anything can seep through walls of a barrier. No containment can keep a substance for too long, or forever. Because that substance will dissipate. It will do what's called a 'switch'.

A switch is to transform: to transform into something else. And so, the 'code switch' that's built into us, that turns our bodies off and on-can also help us seep through the barrier of the exchange.

The exchange represents the bodies movement to escape as in (seep through) its barriers. It gives us the ability and reasons to make our adjustments. Mostly, its because we're trapped.

Exchanges can also exist to other forms and for different substances.

An exchange for 'us,' can represent a foreign body change of introduction into the atmosphere. That should be the only reason why we would develop. We can be developed outside of this so-called petri dish too.

But if we're no longer residing in the petri dish then our substance cannot be contained. Our holding pattern will be free flowing (like the lady that was floating), which was similar to a space mission being completed to capture the body. Neospasms that were introduced cannot be lost. We can be free in a sense but will not become lost. We are only lost in the sense of having to restart. But even that is akin to regeneration.

*(petri dish is being used figuratively to demonstrate the power of what a containment can do)

The design is already prebuilt to make us comeback. But neospasms don't want to lose any parts of their originality and so we get turned off and on in the interim via the switching of our code.

Its debatable, as to what these creatures are. I call them neospasms because if we are their spawns, then they are not really, aliens. We can only call them that (aliens); because they've chosen to let us live outside of their original cell.

There is a source that's called an original cell, which is the master plan of the blueprint of the neospasm.

Neospasms may be many, as in plant, animal, etc. But the original source that provides its makeup can be linked to divinity.

Divinity is the Ultimate Source of our Causation. And thus, divinity holds the 'key' to all, of our patterns.

We don't get to say that there are all of these aliens (foreign bodies) surrounding us and controlling our bodies. It's true that we are their spawns (offshoots), but neospasms also are not the original source.

Divinity (which represents a hierarchy) is the Master of All Domain.

There is dominion over land, water, substance and well...everything. and Divinity is that Source.

What it means to be a part of Divinity is that it gives us our ability to 'code switch'.

Substance

Substance can be in the form of anything. It is also what makes up the body.

Our 'tuning fork' however, has been cast into the spirit. The spirit of an awakening with Divinity.

Bodies can never outlast the divinity source. The source (of the code) that's held within our bodies that leads us to divinity- is done so -for our own sake.

That seems to be the part that we care about the most that is special. There is a special link to Divinity that surpasses the Neospasm.

Neospasms can be viewed as the various shapes and forms that divinity has made to be formed as substance.

Neospasms are original blueprints but all neospasms are coming from Divinity.

Divinity has a dividing line of who and what gets controlled. Spirituality links us in various ways through a series of bypasses.

Signals that are coming directly from divinity can surpass our heritage and lineage structure of the neospasm. Divinity can keep us separated.

The neospasms have introduced us as an induction into our environment, but neospasms knew all along that they must adhere to the masterplan.

We have whats called Divine Purpose. And divine purpose comes from our linkage to within ourselves to understand and connect the code. The code can have barriers but also passages.

The passage is underground, and it is something that should have to 'seep' through (something) to make it escape. Something that's a barrier or containment.

The contract we have is with the neospasms and Divinity. And with us, being the extensions, is why we're controlled.

Causation

Causation is a whole other aspect of what we should be looking at because it is holy.

When Divinity had 'caused' the substance to be formed (as neospasms) there was a linkage that tied them to a contract.

The neospasms are 'US"- that's for sure. But we are their offshoots.

In turn, and likewise-neospasms are offshoots of Divinity which has been born into substance.

The reality of anything- is when we become aware of it. Somehow, we believe that if we can't see it-it doesn't exist.

Most of our iteractions is with the substance because of our linkage to neospasm-but we also have a direct link to Divinity.

When Divinity bypasses the substance from which we are made-that is when we have the ability to transform. The biodegradable substance that gets bypassed is forever exchangeable. Divinity is the only thing that's everlasting.

Neospasms are the chosen tools to have given reasons to substance and to be held and sustained in life's climate. And thus, Causation is an instigation of us living amongst ourselves with these patterns. The patterns that have been chosen for our development.

Cut from The Cloth

We start out as just that. As if we're being cut from the cloth as an offshoot.

If you have ever noticed, there are no new variations. Everything that we see exists in our lifetime.

Cut from the cloth means to 'act' according to the original. We don't even get to change our makeup.

All we can ever do is code switch.

Code switching is coming from the signals. The signals that are held within our bodies. It could be the brain, heart...anything where synergies were developed to keep us alive.

Changing within the pattern doesn't mean that we can change the pattern that we come from. The form from the pattern is set. There seems to be no 'new' originals that are being made.

What we have seen so far is likely all that there are. Changing from within is different. It means that we can switch ourselves on and off from our behavior. We can undergo complete makeovers if we want because internally it would mean that we are changing our characteristics but not what's being controlled.

We have limited capacity, to interact and use our coordination with nature. And we can never reverse course. Not even to go back. We can't revert ourselves back into neospasms that represent our very forms, even if we should come to know about them.

All we can do is 'wait' to be extracted.

But we can 'seep' through the walls that Divinity has left open- that part is reserved.

Divinty speaks to us in ways for us to earn merits. It is through meritorious works that we must part with the neospasms. They care for us and tend to us (unbeknownst to us) and can originate messages- but it is Divinity that sends for us. So it would be divinity that is speaking to us as a large conglomerate of species but the neospasms get to be present.

We can see the birds, the trees, the human forms of our bodies which are designed from a master blueprint. But we are not at the top of the chain.

Our existence is in the chain (of development) is below the original master. The original species from whose 'cloth' we have been cut.

If you don't want to believe this, just look around and 'count' all the original species (of substance) that you can see or figure out.

We're all connected, but we're not the same.

Neospasms have offshoots and we are called spawns- because we have been cut from their fabric or pattern which is a master form of design.

Exchange

The exchange is the reason for our redemption, rehabilitation, and redevelopment. And it is the reason for causation and why we exist.

There would be no reason for us to live if we couldn't go back and be exchanged.

So, change is inevitable whether we can 'seep' through, our substance (as in transforming) or be taken.

If we have 'seeped' through it, we will have died. And thus, our substance turns into gases and dissipates. It dissipates as a form of escape so that it can be returned to the neospasm.

Neospasms are underlings of God. God is at the control of the helm.

There does appear to be an overseer, although I don't know that that means there is just one.

Much of the theories having to do with the concept of One-means that there should have been a start.

Some might say that 'causation' was a result of the inverses having met at some point to form a pattern- a pattern which made substance become as recognizable.

If there were two patterns (coming from both sides) responding negative and positive, couldn't that also be considered as void an non-existent (that which we can't see) having a cataclysmic reaction with what is already present (that we can see) and making and forming a 'new' substance?

Some would say that that is counterbalance and what agitates the initiation of causation.

It is the exchange that tells us our story. If that counterbalance was a predicted model to give off what can be called an explosion of 'causation', then it would be Divinity that caused the disruption...or combustion might be a better word.

I think that regardless of whether we view it as One, one thing causing something- or two-counterbalance of the exchange of opposite forces, we have to acknowledge that the exchange does exist and this is where everything would take place.

We have to be 'taken' back whether our inert gases 'seep' through something or not. We also can be encapsulated (as to form) so that our body is not aware of its transport.

*(I've seen this type of phenomena in action as an actual exchange amongst alien and human passages) it was the observance, that I shared earlier. Something I related also in another book I had written where I give full disclosure as to the context of that observance.)

My observance was as an experience. And has taught me that living through this iteration as visionary, was a supplement to us learning more about ourselves than anything.

Iterations are what we can do as spawns. Experience the changes to our perception to what we can see as a process of development; and when dealing with our behavior.

That is what makes us like tuning forks for all the signals we might receive at some point. The signals that are coming from off of our blueprint that was built into our nature. The code signals are what links us to not only the neospasms, which are master plans of our bodies (predevelopment), but it also allows us to have linkages that can be bypassed with these signals directing us to Divinity.

PART TWO

Some people want to view technology as something strange. They want to go back to their old roots instead of their new roots. This section is about tying technology to our roots.

6 TECHNIFIC!

This part isn't *all* about technology. But it is about some things that are tech related- in a spiritual way.

It's what we should 'want' to know.

Spiritually, we should want to know about these three things related to tech….

-**Intuitive Learning**	-All technology is related; and we can learn by adapting. Its intuitive to see how one thing relates to another, and then continue, on that path.
-**Lifestyles**	-modes: there's modern and old school. Everything that's outdated gets revamped. It also undergoes a facelift-which is a makeover.
-**Our Journeys**	- "A bridge to Somewhere" Click...Click...Click. At the center of our effigy, is the 'human aspect' of pushing a button and we model that behavior.

Have you ever felt like you were out of the loop...like something is just, not, quite right?

Sure, we can push buttons. Now-a-days, they call it swiping.

Swiping with your index finger is like pushing a button into a magic world.

A world where all things can be, "Tech Related".

The button is the interface for opening "the path'

and to make it magical- it must be seamless

Technology has helped us along in many ways. It has become seamless in our daily interactions. We can choose when to use it. Our instincts tell us, that if something looks complicated regarding technology,

we might not want to try it out. That's the 'it' factor of being a robot.

Everything seems robotic now when put into action; and a robot it seems, is something that can change our daily lives.

We can make use of it when its programmable. We get to see and feel its intuitive and adaptive behavior. Much like our own.

Anything can be viewed as a robot.

But let me go back for a minute, to the ones that are really 'old school'. The ones where you could probably still see all the wires hanging out. You would really have to be a 'techy' to approach them.

Most people know that robots can be smart tools to work with because they can intuitively adapt based on programmable behavior. With a button (which is a switch) serving as the interface.

Spiritually, our induction, is as an interface. Like a cars technology that's built right into it. Notwithstanding, that a car has a body (unlike ours), there is still a button that must be pushed to rev it up.

The engine is held under lock and key- meaning that you don't have to know anything about what's underneath the hood to operate the machinery, unless you choose to. You should only have to -push the buttons to make it move and do what it does for you.

Society is built like this; with a happy interface that contains all the toys and gadgets.

And we don't have to ever mind them as being too complicated either as long as they look amazing.

As, long as we are 'happy' with what it does, it becomes less complicated. The interface must be included as the magic button to rev up- so that we don't mind at all.

Intuitive Learning

Learning how things can be related...a wire can be used to connect for example, and solar panels can be used to establish the linkage between the usage of sunlight. A light source that's used could be anything from wires to candles. The wick of a candle (something simplistic) could be viewed as a wire also. However, as ignition, most wires are hidden between walls or connected to lamps. Illumination is the key to what the wick actually- does; and wires also make use of this. If you can compare the two; it is the speed of the wire that would be adaptive.

Coming from both, however...is the light. Which is the purpose, and the key. Our own, intuition, helps us to learn about the sources of the ignition that's coming from illumination as we can view it as helping us to turn something on. Mostly, what we want to do, is push a button. There's heat transfer that's being conducted from the exchange of the wires. There is also a transfer of electricity.

So, the magic, in the wires, as they connect, would be because technology enhances it.

It isn't always, because of the wires conduction, as we can make them seem fancier and have prettier interfaces- (something that seems seamless when it user friendly), technology sells because of its looks. So, everybody might want to have a robot, but they might not want the same one.

We pick our wires as we do relationships in our lives. Based on the way in which the heat is conducted, and cautiously, I might add. So, everything that enhances, may not necessarily be for us. It must be seamless to transfer, so we should have to look underneath the hood to see how the wires are working. There should be some serious thought that goes into pressing buttons. And we shouldn't just press them haphazardly, when they have to do with our lifestyles.

What technology does is adapt to our behavior according to our lifestyles. We will have intuitive responses which makes us different.

There is an effigy in our human knowledge of interactions that goes beyond our images and has to do with our lifestyles. Lifestyles can have predictable outcomes when we base it and rely on technology. But our own independence is tied up in the connections. The connections of what programming does to our succinct and adaptable behavior. Robotic behavior exists because of wiring (whether seen or unseen) but all wiring does is act as a conduit.

The flesh, part of our body, is as a conduit. The wiring that's stemming from underneath is made to adapt and the body's mechanism- produces magic.

Synergies are given off as auras of radiation (which is conduction) every time that we touch something. Thus, we are remitting (just like the wires) our very own illumination.

The synergy can automatically connect and produces a defense shield for anything that's unwanted.

It's like a path that's been chosen as part of a journey.

When heat is conducted there are varying degrees of knowledge that is transferred. Most of it will have to do with what's applicable to our foundation- which are our truths.

So, modernization represents that conduit whereby we can maintain our connections with technology, which produces the same synergies as if coming from us. Emittance and remittance are live streams that go beyond the flesh. While in the meantime. We must maintain, our 'happy interface'.

We are as cushions (levers), which would be like 'root' of a mechanism that would have to be exchanged from time to time to keep it running. Our engine can start from emptiness- a full tank, or in retro, which is reverse. The magic continues to turn us on.

As a conduit- for life- and acting as a heat and energy natural source; we exchange (our bodies) with the atmosphere, as an effigy, which is an image that's long standing. We are magnificently brilliant as technology has lent us our happy interface thereby keeping us attractive where we can be drawn in closer to the source. Together, we push buttons. It's so that we can feel that we have a unique purpose and function. Something that continues to define our development, which is a conduit.

We can have 'heat transference' and, also become our own sources of light as we begin to conduct our experiments into chasing light. Which is intuitive and adaptive behavior given to life as a way of exploration.

We've been transplanted

The human way of looking at it, could be that we use transatlantic exploration. The technology way of showing us that we have been conducting experiments all along is to examine the ways in which we are transported.

Planted in the wombs in the existence of time. This is one way.

Time in which we share a space with something else. Another way.

Intergalactic travel is not new. And we have done this before, with spacecraft. An "old school view', was to look at the stars and count them. So, astrology has played its part. New, school examples, are us, creating our own spaceships.

The one thing I like to share, when telling about my experiences – is that a Spacecraft, or Hover ship, was -definitely, used by outer space beings that have been oriented in our direction. I can- definitely attest to that.

And for all of our experiments that get to be conducted, we don't always get to see them.

We can't see them because the aerospace dynamics makes use of sending signals. Signals that have direct access to our root-which is a lighted source. The lighted source that ignites our bodies happens to be as a cushion- or button. Our body is a happy interface and is user friendly (to these outer space beings). It's done this way so as not to 'scare' us from having all the wiring that's underneath our hoods. So that nothing hangs out or is exposed- its tightly compacted into shape and form. A form of which, comes from the Ultimate Source.

*I've been through a lot of things before as I explained that I had gone through my iterations. I can never tell about something that I haven't personally experienced, or, received through Divine Inspiration. That's what this book is about- me, personally, telling my stories as an Experiencer. So, my visions will dictate the process, and the prose as if...coming from my experience. I'm also a techy person at heart. That's why I've chosen to include that aspect.

Ultimate Source

The ultimate source of our connections as a revelation, is to recognize Divinity.

Divinity is a way of saying that something is working.

Ultimate Source is our bodies lifting- not as in rising; but connecting.

Lifted from a common denominator which is a root.

It doesn't matter what conduit we have; we have been introduced through Divinity. And that is our Ultimate Source.

What is Divine?

Divine, is to experience transference of thought as if it solely resides within our bodies.

Divinity is as an effigy that's at the center of human transfer.

We can 'reach out', to divinity, but mostly it is divinity, that 'reaches in".

It is because we house their spirits.

Home, to us, is a way of seeking to go back.

Neospasms are spawns also, that are generated from the ultimate source of divinity, and it is we, as spawns that imitate their behavior.

A spawn (which can also be us) is born from the flesh and transported through the womb of another person. A neospasm, however, is entirely something else, like a model.

A neospasm is the root of some other form of existence of causation. Something that has occurred over controlling- everything and has taken to us as a lighted source for their extensions.

The spark and ignition of the neospasm is always present. We have to activate the conduit. As spawns we live as if in a chain of events- like having a journey.

The reason that we must understand the Ultimate Source to be as a hierarchy, is because there are varying degrees of knowledge. Each spawn tends to feel out its own source. And that would be more than what's coming from our parents. Neospasms are what we have come from-it's also what we should look like.

We can think that everything is hidden behind the shadows or veil-but it's not. If we look at ourselves closely. We can understand the reasons for our existence.

Most of it is due to having become imprints. We are imprinted from a master plan and blueprint design that can be signaled by the path within our nature. Some of us will never know who we are- we just live. Some will have a closer source- as in connection with divinity. Divinity is in all of us and it is the signal that's used to 'recall'.

Divinity seeks us out through its sources provided to light our path. We do the same. We don't become brilliant overnight; but we are first class citizens. We can have our view of the modern world and at the same time be transported in it.

It won't be as 'modern' all the time. There will be times when we seek to go back to our antiqued ways, however, modernization simply means that you will be given things in the times that you were born. That will be our modern world, and we will advance through it with flying colors even if we feel that we are left behind. This is the known factor about our interfaces. It's that we can be happy using them, because they will feel as modern to us. It wouldn't matter if later generations reflect back and feel as though it is old. So, modern advancements stem from us learning about the 'root' that's coming from ourselves. And that tends to be our greatest enhancement.

The 'root' in the chain as 'tugged' by Divinity through intervention. You can't have a seamless interface unless there are other ways to gain access.

Most of us should be happy to acknowledge that it doesn't require much effort to become tugged at the root. We simply have to reflect.

Neospasm didn't design our purpose but they did use us according to plan.

We don't need a reason to know why divinity exists or the neospasms. What we should know is that everything will go back to its place.

Neospasms don't worry about the aftermath of what it means if we should come to know about them. Any aspect of our ever knowing about them is based on their having full control. Except, for the part that has been reserved for Divinity. Divinity can make use of direct bypass mode at any time.

And the reasons we can't see divinity is because of the root. The root was designed for communication and nothing else. That's why an oratal transcription is taking place at all times and our thoughts (what we're thinking) can be duly noted. It also gives reason and explanation why we tend to function the way we do.

Neospasm are parts of Divinty. It is a wholly (holy) infused transformative operation as a process- that's coming from them.

We go back to them when we're called. And we do this through the exchange.

The root of all of causation is coming from Divinity. We have been pressed through nature and becoming imprints of a divine purpose and plan. Spawns in the chain are duplicated. Neo means newly developed as in wholly (holy) and is a master blueprint that's geared towards returning to its maker as a master designer of the plan.

7 NEVERMIND

God gave us a 'nevermind', so that we shouldn't 'have' to see it *(see something that we should no longer have to worry about). Nevermind, represents the absence of thought. Or, at the very least, trying to correct it.

It's an exchange of worries by replacement, meaning that if you can 'let it go'-it can be as if it wasn't supposed to happen.

Thoughtless memories aren't worries. They have no attachments. This way, you can 'see the best' in everything by adhering to the code. It establishes a creed of forgiveness.

"Never' should you 'mind' that...anymore. Meaning, don't take things to heart.

When we can put something in the background of our memory, as in, 'letting it slide', it is an act pertaining to grace. And that is what God tends to give us-a Graceful exit out of everything-if we choose it.

The order of life is to file things away. Our filing system is such that we can bring things to the forefront of our memories whenever we should need to.

Thus, our bodies respond according to what our memories have taught us. Recollection- means to 'collect' the thoughts that you want to remember- which implies that its hiding in the background.

A 'nevermind' example, is to give that thought back, and to throw it into the junkpile. It should mean that you 'should never' have to engage with it.

We will have 'neverminds' when we leave and depart this life. That is the new understanding. It is that we should have 'never minded' what we ever did because it's not like it will matter later- on. We don't take 'acts of worry' to the grave. We take acts of forgiveness.

Our new business will be to 'nevermind' whatever has happened, because we can no longer engage. Not in the present body. We can only visit after we have left, and it will be our 'grace' to come back to help.

Our 'new' business, once transitioning, will be to 'nevermind' the past. We must recollect and act upon those things while we're here. This will be the only chance we have at making them matter. Thus, our choices are born out of a 'nevermind' set. One that's already been 'set' to forgive. That is how we experience grace also, while we are here- it is through our 'nevermind' sets.

If I'm telling you to forget about it-I'm likely saying, don't let it bother you and/or, that is shouldn't, or no longer counts.

That is the principle of our everlasting, thought provoking- absence of memory skills. Which is not only to erase something, but to delete it.

Memory fades, along with our life (line)-therefore, it wouldn't be necessary to remember those thoughts. We can have, enhanced afterthoughts, after, or during the Exchange. But, at first, our business, is to be blanked out. So that there can be adjustments.

Memory erasure is not permanent immediately, right after death. Purgatory, suspended animation...all thoughtless travel as we 'peer' back through the window.

Our forever holding cell was just a shell. Shells go through what's called, reconfiguration.

*Recalling our past has to do with going forward so that we can 'never be mindful' of what we just did.

That is what the exchange is for. That's why we should have a 'master blueprint'-(neospasm), because, when the body dies-we are presented with a 'never mind' clause that Divinity can erase. It's for our protection.

Imagine taking every burden that we had- with us. We could still be alive in a 'new' form, but worried about the past.

God releases us from that burden and tells us to 'nevermind' once we have passed the stage of no longer needing to recall-our past.

I called it an 'Envelope' that was sealed, in my previous book. I presented it as part of the 'Equation', which showed us our methods or 'mode of living' as we headed for the transition. Recollection was the greatest part of what we could do. But 'nevermind', was to be a fitting ending, to the things we did that were never rehearsed. We couldn't predict, pick out, or rehearse, any of our circumstances. We could only live them out. Viewing them retrospectively, only brought us to the gate. To cross it-as in- being in an Exchange, there was to be a toll.

The toll that you'd pay, was to nevermind' as an exchange, anything what was coming from our past.

The life's, 'flashbacks' happen quickly. Right before you exit. So you can be brought to the gate, no matter what. But to cross it, however, you must 'temporarily' have to nevermind those thoughts.

Full erasure; comes later. Nevermind, is different. It is being thoughtless when 'thoughtless' counts most. Thoughts can be 'whisked away', as in an envelope, while you are being thoughtless.

It is so you can make the decisions to never be mindful again; about anything that's coming from your past.

Helping, means to adhere to the 'code of ethics' that a hierarchy distinctly tells us to follow as part of the conditions of our 'bypass".

Divinity saves us because of Grace, and we, in turn, have to come back to do the same.

Have you noticed that for all that's been done on Earth, a soul, has never come back to get revenge?

It's because we have to 'nevermind' the things coming from our past when we are living as offshoots.

Neospasms don't direct us in this way- they just keep giving us the ability to remake ourselves (as spawns). Divinity takes (extracts), us on to live in a world of 'nevermind' (about the past), in the world of the hereafter.

The' baggage' of remembering, is too great. It is what weighs us down.

That heaviness is why we can never cross the barriers to leave earth.

The barrier is meant to 'lighten our load' as we go through it-which is...the Exchange. We can 'help' others who are fulfilling their dreams- but we can never take revenge out on others. We can, however, stop-certain actions. That is something we will have the ability to do.

No souls go on to worry. No souls can ever go on to the transition without having to 'nevermind' the things coming from their past.

Remembering everything- if you can, is before you can cross over.

Experience; means nothing. You can either leave as mature, immature, or even as premature.

-immature means you never have developed (much)

-premature means that you were in the process of learning

-mature means that you understood some things more or less, based on exposure- which often means longevity and that you have lived a longer life.

When we are 'taken' as in extracted from our living quarters; you can experience things such as I had. You can be 'shown' an 'otherly' world, in operation, without dying.

You can be taken as either- young, old, or an adult.

Prematurely, meant that it happened abruptly, so you will not have completed the full life cycle.

Nevermind, is absence. It is absence of thought (through memories, right before it's going to be erased.

If neospasms become transplanted, even if they share the bodies of new forms, usually its's when life was taken abruptly. Then coming back as a newborn, doesn't shed all the memories because you'd likely have to be born fast.

If you've completed your life cycle at the mature stage of development, you likely get to become an elder...that gets closer to the blueprints.

If they can keep you at that stage-from going back-then you are spared.

That is our heavenly transition. We call heaven a place of peaceful abode-this is why.

There is more risk with maturity passing than there is with a death that was premature (such as a child).

The passion of life still exists, and it must be decided at the exit-what must be dispensed with.

New Bodies-

New Forms-

Master Plans-

Master Exhibits-

All are in Heavens' path.

When we mature and die-Divinity decides what part of us stays. We would have to adhere to a 'code of ethics' when we're brought forth. So as not to have to 'test' us-they (Divinity), makes it so that we can 'nevermind' whatever it is that we did.

Thoughtless methods were 'chosen' to be used for transitioning. Otherwise, when we left (departed) we'd continue our old grudges.

This is the Ultimate in mind control and that's the part that's being done as a 'code switching'. Divinity's direct line that can penetrate the Neospasms current shell that it's using as spawns.

There's never too many to watch and extract because of this code.

The Ultimate Question then, is...Who has made the Makers?

This, I believe-no one can answer.

Maybe by my next book, they will have let me know.

I do know that it will have to do with substance. Substance, as we describe it-can also appear-as nothing.

FIXATION

Sometimes, we can be fixated with things...but we don't know why.

What's your Driver?

My driver was that I just wanted to know the truth (about many things) and I've been struck, with the 'fixation' of what that 'truth' is. IJ

We have different drivers. We have different motivators. Some things that are key to our understanding- about anything, is what's driving us or motivating us to do it.

I had a conversation with my granddaughter's friend. He had just completed thirteen days of meditation. He went into the complete darkness for thirteen days without any contact or social interactions. While he just happened to share this with me (and I know nothing about his journey), when he came out, or emerged as we called it, we were happy to see that he had made it-safely out of his personal conquest.

Before he went in, he had wanted to be sequestered. So, we had this conversation about it when he happened to stop by with her, while my granddaughter was visiting me. In his excitement, from just having completed his quest, he had wanted to share.

I noticed that he had lost a lot of weight and he said he really hadn't been eating, especially the last five days. He began his conversation with recollecting his thoughts about what he had seen and experienced in the darkness. He had gotten through a couple of his episodes when I paused-or stopped him to ask him a question.

"What is you end-game?"

I posed this question not out of curiosity, but with a real concern of wanting to know what it is that he was trying to achieve. And if it was nothing, that was fine too.

I wasn't trying to steer or redirect the conversation. I just sincerely, wanted to know.

He interrupted the excitement in which he had become enthralled behind telling his initial story about his quest-to switch gear as an attempt to give me an answer. He began to tell another story. One that he thought, was probably not related.

He mentioned a very horrific accident, where he said that his father (intentionally) crashed a car (with him in it) into a wall.

This would obviously be a traumatic experience for a small child, so I listened intently.

"We crashed into the wall of a hospital, and then I saw a light flash."

He was using his crystal rocks to demonstrate after telling me this.

I observed his lineup of the rocks as he took one figure and placed it on the floor saying, 'this was the end'. Another he had placed right after with only few spaces between saying, 'this is the beginning'. Then he took a sphinx shaped rock, or crystal that he had in his hand, and moved it towards the other two rocks he had placed, saying that this was where he was headed. That he was trying to get to the beginning. The beginning to him, was the second rock he had placed. So, I coyly sat and watched his actions and humbly tried not to reach any conclusions as to my own understanding of what those rocks meant. I merely observed.

What was his driver? That was the question I had posed to him before he told me the story about him and his dad's accident. The first question I had asked him even before that was, 'what was his endgame?'

He also had mentioned, while demonstrating with the rocks that were lined up in front of both of us on the floor; that he was trying to 'go past' the ending. Which to me, meant that there was a reference or implication of death, or the possibility of meeting (death) at some point...in order for him to continue...to get to the beginning. And while he never used the word (death) while discussing this, but the inference, to me, was there and pretty scary. That's why I was having a conversation with him. To get to the bottom of what his drivers could be, and also his end game, which could have to do with what he expected to get out of it.

I thought that it was an interesting story. So, I premised, my response based on what he had demonstrated with his answer.

What I shared with him based on my observance and him telling me the facts behind his accident, is that I could 'kind of see' what his drivers might be and also his endgame towards his goals and objectives for wanting to meditate in complete darkness for 15 or more days.

This opened up a whole new conversation consequently, of something that I had learned about myself. I mentioned it earlier, about the little girl running away. It's something that I knew innately, and had written about several times in the past, but because of this conversation with him, I had now, given it more credence based on having a new context.

So I started my response out by telling him...*based on what you have said...*

"Your drivers seem to be that you might be having a 'fixation'. Your fixation is that you are wanting to see what was on the 'other' side of the light. You know that something had saved you (both him and his dad) because you could have been killed in the car crash, and whatever it was, you didn't get to see it.

The wall that you crashed into could be what's standing between and/or blocking you from your observance. So, I think that maybe, ever since a child, when that happened, you have been trying to get back to the beginning...starting from the end. The beginning for you, was before this crash ever happened, when everything was still, ok. So, the beginning could represent being safe, as in ok.

You also could be contemplating about the fact that this could have been pre-meditated (by your father) which means that the crash would have been intentional. The trauma that's stemming from that experience could be why you're looking for your answers. So, meditating completely in the dark- was one form of you trying to discover the light. And the light could really mean to you-what it is that was behind it (as you were a young child) in that crash, when something had saved you.

You might somehow (subconsciously) feel that you have 'cheated' death because you weren't supposed to make it. But...somehow, in that flash of light- that could have been that dying moment, the moment that was the end, you were saved. And so from there...was your 'new' beginning. However, trying to wish that things had never happened, you have perpetually been seeking the 'crossing' of the barriers, that's been pertaining to that light.

While I'm no psychologist, I told him. I offered my conclusions of this as likely being his driver.

A driver is something that can be seen, as a motivator. A motivator for our behaviors. And his behavior-had been taking him on a quest. That is what led him to maximize the extremes of meditating under increased and added pressure of doing it in the dark. To me, it was his quest to find his light. That light he had experienced stemming from that traumatic experience.

He said that he had learned something when I told him all of this. Explaining it in such a way so as to not necessarily be teaching him, but to have shared it as my observation as in forming an analysis-and opinion.

Only he-himself, can know what his inner- most thoughts are. But I did share with him that my explanation of this was also from having watched him and my granddaughter's journey and experiences that they've taken together involving rocks and crystals. Both of which I know little about, except that they each place a great deal of faith in them. So, his demonstrating while using them would not be unusual, but it did seem out of the ordinary how he had placed them while trying to give his answer. That's what drew my attention even more so than what he said.

I'm not a disruptor. I don't consider myself to be the type of person that tries to dissuade someone from anything I might consider unusual (such as always having or using rocks and crystals) as a way of completing their quest. As long as something isn't detrimental, I don't necessarily see the harm as long as things aren't taken to excess. Rocks and crystals can have meanings, I understand that. But it wasn't for me to pass judgement even if they don't align with my own views. It's about placement. Not passing judgement. If he hadn't demonstrated (how he felt) with those examples given from his rocks...I might not have ever understood the important connection they had to his quest.

But it was my place, to share my Experiences and Observations that I felt could be related-If, in fact, I was to be blessed enough, to have insight. It doesn't mean that something is true or not true. I felt compelled to share my thoughts with him about what could be driving his quest. I also know that for many people, it's not always that simple. An explanation given at a casual glance, can be offered as an observation. However, the parent-child relationship that's dormant inside of many of us that seems to be locked inside -can affect us throughout our life. Especially, if its traumatic. But there also could be many other factors.

With me uncovering and unlocking his story- I was able to make inroads into my own. And it made me reflect upon what could be my very own drivers as well.

As a child, I told him, as I continued...I always used to run away from stuff- whenever there was discord.

If there was fighting or arguing within my family for instance, my solution, was to run away.

Or, if I could at least 'threaten' to run away, maybe someone would notice...and that would stop the fighting.

It never worked. And no one did really notice or pay attention to what I was doing. They were too caught up or intent in doing whatever it was, to pay attention to a little girl crying out because of seeing her family members in a brawl. So, my anguish had begun while I was very, young too, I had told him, and it stemmed from family related trauma.

Whenever I'm faced with chaos (as a means of coping- I try to 'stop it' by threatening to remove my presence. It's as if I'm so worthy and important, that I feel I can be the 'lone stopper' since someone would care so much. It's also because I was hurting from the pain and anguish of the feeling of someone getting hurt- so much so, that I didn't want that to happen. I wanted there to be peace, and for everyone to get along. This happened a few times that I can recall and over the course of the years, I had threatened to run away -and no one would notice. So I'd run off half-baked, as they say- not really having a backup plan. I would only want to distance myself temporarily, but at the same time to return when all was well, and everything had subsided.

I shared this with him (my granddaughter's friend), as a way of explaining how I had come to understand my own drivers regarding my quest. I further explained that... I didn't necessarily have a quest, as I can see it through observation, but more or less was me, avoiding something. Avoiding anything that was with turbulence; that could ensue. I said to him that I had never personally sought to discover or join with anything pertaining to the light. And that mine could be seen as an 'act of avoidance'-unlike him who was headed directly into it.

I told him that I have seen light too, but in a different way. And although intrigued-I didn't seek to head toward it intentionally.

I explained that 'light' has been shown to everyone and everyone can see it in some capacity and in some way. What we do with any aspect pertaining to light will be based on our experience.

My quest was only for the truth. The truth about Everything. And I didn't choose to run towards the light in that regards, I only acted in the moment of what was brought to me. There is a difference between 'seeking' and experiencing. As a seeker, you will have-what you have sought out with the end- result, still not known. Meditation is one form of seeking. And for many, it works.

I discovered (as I continued telling him my story in response to him telling me his), that uncovering my drivers, as part of my motivation as it pertains to anything that leads to a quest, had to do with my 'flight and risk' syndrome that I had experienced as a child. So just like him, who experienced something dramatic (stemming from his childhood), I had too. Only I had taken mine a step further (subconsciously) by running away from it.

Seeking truth and going to the light after having observed the 'flash' as he put it, can lead to very, different ways of the acceptance of what that pursuit is.

I saw it as the 'light coming to me' and although I may have 'asked' questions leading up to it, my encounter with it (I may have been engaged in prayer at the time-etc.), I never wanted to know...what else, was out there, as in, what else, could be lurking beyond the light.

I've always been a faithful person that believed we have helpers. But it was the many dreams that I had throughout the years that helped me realize that everything pertaining to the light shouldn't be sought. So instead of leaning towards it- (my inner child) made me chose to run away. Yet...and still...it always came back-to me. I had a fixation with truth-not necessarily, the light.

The light might represent that 'flashing' moment before our eyes when you can observe whatever it is; or see the action that could be saving you. But 'light bulb' moments happen to us all the time. Some pertaining to good, and bad situations. I only want to know the truth. So, seeking truth has been my fixation. And it wasn't because of me heading towards or wanting to see what was on the other side.

I'm an Experiencer.

And with experience comes a bit of maturity. We experience things at different ages whether immature, mature or premature-all at times when we can be randomly 'taken' as well.

What we are being 'taken' too, whether its abrupt or not, is to be shown the light. Which is also to be on the 'other side' of our quest.

I told him, that since this is where we're headed anyway, and that it also could happen at any time, 'why not just appreciate the fact that something was there to save you?' So you don't have to expedite any passageways or openings to go and find out what the savior is. You will find out anyway...maybe, in due time.

So, I don't personally head towards the light.

I don't pursue or ascertain anything as far as an opening.

Anything that I've learned, said, or done, in that regard, has been from my Experience.

I've experienced 'crossing' because I was taken (it wasn't by choice- I didn't seek it).

I've had dreams- (because something that was there, used that medium, as a form of communication).

I've been given 'gifts' of clairvoyance (which is to see things ahead) although I never asked for it-nor could I ever prevent anything as a result of it.

And I never once, wanted to pursue anything related to chaos. Perhaps, as my chosen method- stemming from childhood, I would do the exact opposite and run away from it.

So, we complete our quests differently. Sometimes we may never know that we're even on a quest.

A quest; is to question. And you get to do this through your very own observation. That observation-or techniques used to uncover the things stemming from our past to be used as drivers or motivators are likely done so subconsciously. That's why, in some cases, we could never fulfill them.

I still have that 'scary' inner child deep inside of me. This disposition of mine has never changed. I also, know now, that it has been what has been driving my 'fixation'. My fixation with discovering the 'truth' about -our paths in life and situations. I always wanted justice and peace and to no avail, I am a seeker of that. And it was behind the light pertaining to that; that the light has come to me.

We can amplify what's hidden deep inside without knowing. My granddaughter's friend may not have known his end game nor his drivers. But as a result of my experiences- I've discovered mine.

Fixation is a way of us -sorting out and finding the paths to our truths.

Fixation is to store all the images that we've ever seen and felt and having them come through as our motivators or drivers. It is beneath the layers that we search for ourselves and that is why we seek what's inside. Truth can be unknown to others. All we can do is share what we experience and what we know. For myself, it was Divine Wisdom that gave me a bigger purpose, even if I didn't want it. It's mostly because I try to dispense with anything that's associated with chaos. But it was through and via the chaos that I found my truths- even as I chose to run away. Truth -or the discovery of it- has now become my very own fixation.

*So, we all will have fixations in some form. Sometimes leading to a quest. Whether they are from using rocks, crystals (like my granddaughter and her friend), or many other things that we find as necessary ingredients to enhance our calling and give us capabilities for finding what truly matters to us most.

The reasons we have 'fixation' is because of the flow of energy that's a directional pull to the centrifuge. And this usually involves and pertains to what matters on the 'other side' of the light.

Fixation- is to 'fix' something that's been broken or can either serve as a link.

8 EARTHS LINKAGES ARE KNOWN BY DESIGN

Earths Links are what develops our formations. I've included my own drawings as a Divine Example of Earths linkages capabilities to our Fixations. *(reference drawing on back pages)

We like to use the reference of Earthlings. I call us 'Earth linkages to the centrifuge' which was divinely inspired.

What's different about the centrifuge is the 'blast' and the 'split'. Its viewed as coming from the earths central core (see diagram in back). However, my diagram in back shows the directional flow of what rebounds when there are fixations. There are sectional and pivotal points on everything that has linkage to the centrifuge. A centrifuge can be rotational in both spirit and effigy (like a fan), so it is not coming from us (meaning ourselves), it is coming from our dwelling. Images rebounding outside of their holding source (which is a shell) as a means of providing us with a linkage. Each, and every object has transportable material that can be transposed into any position. We would have to clarify (for clarities sake) which object it is we're trying to 'pull' from. Earth will give us our linkages, as long, as, the centrifuge holds. Once the core has been disrupted, and sections divided, every 'fixation' that we have will leave our inner space on its own, thus, us seeking a quest- becomes mute, in itself. There is no such fixation that can be everlasting. It is only our pivot points and spirits traveling out of bounds that control whatever it is around it. That's a natural, phenomena that's occurring, so anything that we touch or feel its presence can essentially become our fixation.

I seek to discover truth on its own which carries its own light. And not necessarily the means of any transport which could be from the use of materials. That's not to take away from any brilliance that can be gained from appreciating anything that's close to or has linkage to the centrifuge. There is 'charm' in everything. But there also is 'harm' in somethings to.

This is how Earth and our linkages to it, can work:

We think that we live on the surface. But it is because everything is 'planted' that we can continue our growth. So, earth was made in such a way that everything could be planted. This happened over and over. If we ever are to leave this earth, we lose our weight and become lifted. It's because we will lose our bodies; and our bodies design, is to be filled. An effigy is our bodies figure or form. Like an image or model- the synergizes through 'code switching' (which happens above ground), Divinity's linkage is into our spirit. And I don't know everything about what Divinity does, I can just relate the message about the Neospasms that have been designed to become earth deposits.

So, the earth was built first- but the reason for ever building earth and us having linkages to it-are unknown.

We're not 'from the dust'. We're 'of the dust'. The dust, like the water, will never leave this earth. When we emerge (inertly) through inertia, the imagery is already known and held fast. That part, we don't see. The protection of our bodies- Seeing is Believing-remember? Isn't that what we said from the start?

Remember that what you 'see' and 'realize' can come into actualization. And actualization leads to this revolution of what's called 'causation'. We didn't come about as a 'root' to discovery. We came about as an everlasting and forever 'being' that seeks the directional pull from the overflow of what was planted. We have always been 'pressing out' of things. Even our situations. We can continue to live in life's form as humans as long as we remain as outstretched and outgrowths of our everlasting image. Whatever earth contains gets agitated. Agitation leads to the cells developing lasting relationships that are lasting bonds with centrifuges of all natures through its link. Earths stages is as a centrifuge of all development and we ourselves are linked to the Divine.

Since we were not made here- things planted that give us life are here to serve as our foundation. Our leakage (linkage) through transport (which is formed by liquid and gases) is to plan our escape. However, we can never go anywhere, we just get tweaked back into our foundation.

That doesn't mean we don't leave. It means we will always have a bond to the foundation for which we were made.

The spiritual realm of the exchange is for the Absence of Thought. It is where we are predisposed to become disconnected. Turned 'off' and 'on' as part of the exchange- is more accurate.

Dust serves as centrifuge of inorganic materials that can sustain the substance of an 'instance' that was created. Molding and shaping, comes naturally, when it applies to dirt. However, pre-configuration of life forms are patterns of composition. The dirt is a catalyst, everything is set from it, but dirt, alone, can't fix, repair, or rejuvenate any type of substance that's already been created. We can rebound from earths centrifuge based on the synergies it possesses in relation to other inorganic materials. Being sculpted as an impression, didn't come from dirt. It was formulated by a neospasm as if pressed from a mold. "Of the dirt' but not 'from the dirt' means that we were pre-molded ahead of time to be sent as earthly deposits. Our growth is paramount and parallel to everything that earth does. That's the centrifuge.

Exchanges are all around us. It takes the exchange to manipulate the substance. Bodies that pass through the exchange are designed to 'code switch'. Code switching is like dialing into us counterclockwise. It's because everything needs to be rearranged to accommodate the switching that takes place when we are -communicated with, for example. Divinity dialing is like a 'tapping'. Sometimes you'll hear the sounds of inordinate matter seeping through your conscious and other times it could be explicit behavior to get your attention. I know that communication is done through code switching because we can't turn ourselves off and on. We also can't rearrange what's outside that's coming in. the ultimate exchange is patterns of code switching that's done above and beyond us. No matter how much time we spend through meditation and other forms of inward reflection, it's beyond our ability to escape the dust unless we're being 'tapped' as a resource. A summoning, of sorts, to get our attention. Also, to prepare us for next steps as to entering the exchange. Our bodies can last as an impression of an imprint of whatever neoplasmic form of life that has given us 'spinoff'. It has to do with vertigo aligning which makes us stand upright as opposed to crawling on all fours. The plasmic- compound inserts via cosmic forces. Our bodies don't seem to last that long, but the figures do. Our lasting impressions have to so with our existence. Existence in this life form as we're holding cells for heavenly- origination in all aspects. Even if we take up a God complex relative to our positioning as a so-called 'superior' being. We can't exchange or substitute the material that made us. We only exist as duplication through spawning. That's the closest we can get to recreating something on our own.

Causation creates a backlog of life forms. Existence is necessary to master the configuration. We exist to join life forces in a way that enhances the exhibit in which we live. However, Divinity can tap into us at any time.

Retraction

When people say you are retracting from them (as in detracting), you literally are probably doing that. Depleting their resources, that is-or what they might deem as valuable. The world is not bent on us making our errors and mistakes. It is bent because we can go through the exchange.

Retraction-as in The Rubberband

I always knew that we had to sacrifice. I just didn't know what it was. We often have to 'give up' something, so that we can 'get' something else. This sacrifice is known as an Exchange. An exchange is happening all the time around us -but this part is due to no fault of our own. Someone must have learned the meaning of sacrifice at some point to be able to apply it as a ritual. Placement, or replacement does occur. Giving up something for something else-is not new.

What's new, is learning about it in a different way than what we know. As divinity strikes, I listen. Then I pass it on. There is what's called a 'rubberband effect', whereby retraction of something is done in exchange (as in performing a ritual) only this ritual isn't being performed by us. There also isn't a requirement for us to participate. The extent of our own participation would be as 'wanting' something. It's to want something so bad that not only would we pray about it, but ask of it-as if something would need to happen.

The exchange gives an unknown distribution allowance although sometimes we might think it's unfair. Nothing is spared, because all that exists must play its part. Asking, is merely the beginning or the onset.

Divinity has rules for how we should live in our abode. I often talk about how divinity 'strikes' as in sparing us, or either giving us what we want. Sometimes, I think it's like a toll- this subtraction mechanism that takes place when the lever is pulled. Its pulled by the asking, need, and our wanting something so bad that it must be switched out.

A fee is being paid by our debt. It's like a double entry fee however whereby we give, and we take. The rubber band retracts and expands until it bounces back. The rule about self- sacrifices is that what you give or get, will be unknown. The quality of the distribution within the network of sacrifice is that Divinity takes away something that's considered to be comparable. At this point I am only talking about the *effects* of rubber band expansion not necessarily what it is that can or needs to be sacrificed.

If you pray for someone to heal- the rubber band retraction says that someone else might get sick. And if the illness was so severe that they might be in a position to pass (as in die) then your praying (as in asking) could reverse the course , however the exchange (of a body) might need to be swapped.

I witnessed this in action once and was convinced that self- sacrifice (as a ritual) is coming from divinity which has a stake in allowing things to reverse course. An exchange as a life for a life-has happened. And I don't mean peoples contrived conceptions of doing these types of rituals personally. I think that would be disgusting to try to circumvent what occurs naturally. And that's my personal opinion on the subject matter. I've come to know about self-sacrifice based on natural occurrence and how we were born. We can live through some things but not others. We can also be 'saved' from ourselves without ever knowing. Whatever warrants it, is not for us to talk about, its for us to be grateful. What I've come to know is that the Exchange can be swift. It is also NOT performed by us. We can never switch as in code switch what is being swapped.

I also think that it's sad. I get my divine inspiration- but then, I *have to* ---deal with its consequences. The consequences that it brings based on understanding. Its uncanny how it works. There is no opportune time to be swiftly taken away. There is only the exchange being offered for the exchange of souls. You don't have to be satisfied with this explanation. It took me awhile myself to grasp it. Rubberband effect means that something giveth and taketh and gets set back to its original course no matter how much upset it caused. I can promise you one thing regarding knowing about this...and that is that it must be a ritual that we practice over and over. Clearly some of us will recognize it, some of us won't.

"Once, I had prayed for a dear relative to be healed. Another was swiftly taken".

There are no bounds to the exchange, and it doesn't always give us what we want. Having fixations with objects is futile. The real intent is what counts. I didn't have to think long or hard about how its connected. I only had to blink once to understand. Its as if something was given to me in a flash of light.

This one isn't too hard to figure out if you've had the personal experience of having something swapped.

***

There is another aspect to Rubber Band that is a little less known even more so than switching or swapping souls in the interim of asking or getting something that you want.

This one is a little 'deeper' and might require some 'soul searching' to understand.

I almost didn't want to admit grasping this one. It has a little 'touchy' feely' aura about it when it involves people that you love.

There's pain that I felt deeply when I had to learn about 'snatching'. Its similar in technique to swapping and switching, however it is much more intensive because it is something that you must live through.

The exchange offers us one way to reach back at someone. But also, randomly, there is self- sacrifice when its being done through the bloodline. So, sacrifice is not a ritual that's being done by divinity as a clearing house to ultimately meet its quota (as if I know if it has one). But there must be some kind of deal that's made for switching to occur in the first place. I wrote about this earlier, in one of my books when I had made a reference to 'kooks'. It was called, "When Crows Call". Written about my episode while staying in a convalescent home while having my experience with a nurse.

In life, we can experience many things. One of them is learning. There can be exceptional and phenomenal growth when it comes to us applying what we can learn. In regards, to methods...well, that's another thing.

We can actually- 'lose' our minds at random and unwarranted. We could also experience a permanent disposition as to having lost what we already know. Divinity gives us 'temporary insanity' to sometimes save us. It could sometimes be as a blessing or as a curse. But it will always have to do with sacrifice.

If you are big on learning, circuited wires can be shut down. They can also be expanded. The rubber band will giveth and taketh until it maximizes it output and extensions. What we lose is a 'part of our being'. That's an expression. An expression of saying that if something is being detracted, as in retracted, then there would be compensation. Our brains are set to learn but the average brain needs to be recharged. There can be a random and selected few among us that reach full capacity with all of the wires.

Wisdom is very profound and with it comes consequences just as in wanting something. If Divinty has chosen to make an opening for your growth, something else must be sacrificed. What I have discovered is that it usually is in the same chain or lineage. If someone is given (knowledge) abundantly, spiritual or otherwise, there will be someone along the chain that its either taken away from (detracted) or what they already know has been stopped.

I've literally seen this take place in my line of descendants. It may have been that I was overloaded so much myself that detraction never occurred to me. Not in the sense of using the word- self-sacrifice. It's not that we can't be born with learning difficulties, because we can. It's that the 'toll' that's given for being a recipient of Divine inspiration for example-requires a fee. The fee is that 'for all that you know and receive as a gift-someone else might not ever get the chance.

I've seen where someone can be so smart and overachievers, and then what's passed down, is the opposite.

It's because of the rubberband.

Some of you may not want to acknowledge this, but I've seen where much was given and then through genealogy, it was lost. It's the same principle working as with the swapping when you are asking for something. Someone to be saved, for example. The exchange allows for some folks to forget that they ever knew anything. It brings it back to the light of the foundation where everything is set. If you can pull a plant, then another one grows. But sometimes that new growing plant, might not reach the light of day. It can be stymied by its growth and there's no guarantee of it ever reaching its full apex or potential. Lost, is one way of putting it. But retraction, is another. Sometimes we can be so blinded in following the light (of some source) that we forget to nurture the ones that can come after us. We also might have to live with them (as our loved one) never grasping or reaching their full potential. Through no fault of our own the division is split. Sometimes 50/50, sometimes equal lateral as in a kid can suffer versus an adult.

We all know that the rate and speed of individual growth is unequal. But wisdom is born- as in hatched, from its holding cell of clarity. We can 'function' with our brains, but our paths can be blocked, halted, or stilled. You are NOT detracting personally from a descendant. It's that the exchange acts as if, from time to time we must allow this as an offering. The rubber band takes no prisoners, it stretches until it reaches a comparable position and then it retracts. So, it has never been about the mistakes, or errors, it's about the compromises that we're willing to put up with. There are reasons given in which we can 'crack' under pressure. But there are also reasons that are unknown. The rubber band has a part in giving and taking when it comes to knowledge and growth.

That is also why we could never just be all spiritual.

Again, I can only talk about what I've experienced. It's not that I've seen people being halted. But I have seen them reverse course. There's a lot of pressure that we're under when it comes to the rubber bands effect. Push and pull, is almost like in and out, however, we live through it as we compromise. Someone in our heritage or lineage will likely suffer if you are given the gift of brilliance. It's as if you are taking away from their light because there's not enough to go around. And that would be the saddest part. So, retraction from the rubber bands effect is real. It's a real as anything else that we experience in the exchange.

Maybe we shouldn't be so hard on ourselves when we can't think, or there's blockage. If we're being 'shut down,' its likely automatic. Everyone will experience some sort of disconnecting as far as our growth. But when we are stunted its likely coming from the root and may be temporary or permanent. The same degree or caliber that you can grow, can be the same one that detracts. Offshoots, by nature, are planted via the exchange according to their roots. The roots of lineage and heritage.

I can say that right now my roots have been in overload and the rubber band keeps expanding. I can't help but wonder if it will 'stop' at the other end when someone I love will be affected.

What's given to someone, can also be taken away from someone else. This I am astutely aware- based on my experience.

When we are replacing the rules- we tend to set out our own objects for worship to help us along with our suffering. Not realizing that all along - Divinty had a plan whereby it didn't require us to be given updates. Downloads, yes. As I explained earlier in my tech talk related to things being programmed. It is through iterations that we can learn about what makes the trade- offs. Some (in our lineage) will suffer more and be lost as to their experiences. I sometimes feel guilty and partly responsible when I've been selected. Guilty is an understatement when it comes to Divinty overloading us with the things we should want to know but don't necessarily 'need' to know. That's why we don't have to be- all the way spiritual. This line of succession thing, as it's called- really does work like a rubber band retraction whereby some will be given, and some will be taken. It's not always up to us what we should know. Divinity acts on our behalf after we have started or revved up the engine. There are different forms and levels to everything. That's why most of what I've experienced spiritually and otherwise, has been through a series of graduations.

Summation

Creation was born of itself. And you might have your own thoughts about it, but that's' my take on it.

It didn't require our 'makers' to bring existence. Makers brought 'causation".

They established the causes to our 'modes of living' and required us to abide by them.

Creation was a 'flash of light' much like the combustion theory I presented earlier.

The thing about creation is that it was oral- meaning 'spoken' into existence. What's created, were the sounds. Body forms came after.

*Preexisting meant that thoughts were free flowing and absent substance. Substance then became eyes, ears and a mouthpiece. That's what we all have in common (all creatures). It isn't necessarily our shapes and forms.

"I was walking through a path with my two granddaughters. On the other side of the hill, there was water. And there were lots of people there – as far as you could see; but you had to get past the tall trees and bushes.

I ran into something out of the ordinary. When I looked ahead; while walking the path, I could see, a large eagle just standing. It was about ten feet away. I told my granddaughters 'don't go near it' because-if it can be this close to people on the ground, it's either sick, or injured.

They were curious just as I was, but I visibly made the gesture in front of the bird to not be a threat. I told them that we should walk to the side to appear as if not to be heading towards it.

It was a s if I had met an 'Element of Equal Power" but knew that we shouldn't be in the same space.

That bird had obviously chosen to fly down for a reason since it knew it could be taking chances (only hidden slightly), by the bushes.

As we veered to the right to avoid it -it spread its wings slightly and hopped a few feet away from us but didn't take off. This was a huge bird, somewhere around the size of a toddler-it looked as it was standing.

My granddaughter was taking pictures and I reminded her not to frighten or follow it. She responded, 'I don't think that it's injured. I think it's something else.'

I could see that it was holding something underneath its huge claws. It was an animal. A very, large squirrel that it obviously had used its laser eyes-with precision, to come down to get.

There were squirrels all over the park and they weren't afraid to come around people. This area was somewhat isolated; except for anyone that wanted to take a shortcut to get to the water-which was us.

I don't think we could have seen this any other way-not up close and personal.

The eagle-being in its own element-reminded me that its "blueprint' was powerful. Here we are as two...no three, entities that could meet-in an unlikely place (after all this was a public park heavily trafficked, except for maybe a few woods that folks might happen to venture to seldom and randomly.

The eagle was caught in the act. And it didn't fly off because it didn't want to lose its prey. So, it stood there with the squirrel underneath its claws that you could barely see. It reminded me of how many Blueprints there are-that could be out there. And that each-is powerful in its own element.

It also reminded me that there was something more to nature-and the way it was planned- that we could ever know about.

I was supposed to 'mind' my own business and be grateful that the eagle minded its own too, since, with its large size- that it didn't target a kid.

This reminded me to be grateful-that creators (as makers), have chosen, through 'origination', to keep us separated.

All neospasms don't get to go back directly to God. They weren't created All at once, but might likely be from one source, so that they can serve as a model for a blueprint.

There will be impressions of everything; expressly designed as imprints, to keep this thing going.

So, design, and creation, are separate. So, much so, that an Original Source, could mean that we weren't created, all at once.

Because we do all have similar forms of communication, as far as connecting because of the 'code'. We each, however, must live in our own element. That's why I have said that- 'not too many more blueprints have been produced (as in introduced) as of late. There are only the ones we can see. A powerful, Being, doesn't have to make itself. It is remade. And remade as spawns to continue to live.

If we never saw each other, (us and the bird), or crossed paths...whatever we each did, in life-would not matter.

Creation came about as visual-it is a present, set of conditions.

Anything can be formed from life, but it is life, that gives us our forms. Forms of Existence.

Everything else was created off, of that.

So, the ANSWER to our ONE BIG QUESTION of what, or who is the Ultimate Source? It would be to wonder 'why' a source should ever begin.

And after studying all the signs- I guarantee you that your answer will be –NEVERMIND.

It's because you are Supposed to Forget about it-even if you had the chance to ever know.

There's void-and avoidance. Just like I did with the bird.

That bird stood there reflecting in its own element, as I projected mine.

Neither of us, had the forethought of why each other exists.

That I would be cognizant of the bird, lets me know that 'each' in its 'element', happens to exist-as part of the Exchange. And all barriers to cross, meant that, reminding ourselves (of our stories) through recollection, is something that we do while alive. To cross the barrier- we must void it all out, and see it presented again.

That is Creation- and also what it means to be Created.

The barriers of existence-exist in our minds, and we should have to follow them. The only thing we should need to know about creation, is that it is to no longer to exist.

Which means that- as a 'thought' about creation-it just wasn't there.

To not exist means that there is- a void-in us.

So, creation, however it came about (into existence), was from a void. A void of the absence of thought- which is 'not knowing'.

God, to us-is 'Not Knowing'.

Not knowing that an 'Original God' exists in any form except to be VOID.

That is perhaps-Origination- an agitation of Causation.

What we know to be void is Sound, -soundwaves that travel as preexisting thought.

Thought that has been agitated to result from interaction with substance.

This world matters. And it matters because- everything that we do, will be what we know.

But, what if we 'don't know' anything?

Matter just hasn't been stirred.

We come into the world as- visual-and hearing sounds. To avoid this wouldn't be part of our nature.

This agitation, and interaction, is the means by which, everything has come into its own. On a course that's been predesigned.

You can't make the track without the cars-or the people in them (or controller mechanism-to drive). But you can make all courses the same -

according to the design. Meaning that you should have to either fly or walk.

So, there is the sky which gives us space. There are the seasons-whose courses are preset. There are the thorough ways that we can make such as meeting the eagle that happened to be in my path. And there are the obstacles, of interacting through the exchange of our bodies with something that was chosen to be in the way.

The Ultimate Source- is something that just wasn't there. Not only void- but, as a magical erasure. And when I say 'there', I mean, 'just not seen'.

That is the Ultimate Source. It is to be able to show up anywhere, at any time and to be anything-because it can.

Life chooses an abode first and then came creation of the neospasms, to begin as blueprints and then to become spawns to continue.

The stellar galactic forces that surround-suppress the life forms mechanism, as a, means to discover, the VOID of life, other than to experience it as coming from death. Which is displacement.

What we should know is that Divinity has chosen for us to live in a way that provides access to something that's called- -Origination.

9 ROADMAP

My very own Pictionary

***(reference pictures in back that depict some of the scenes, places and spaces in which most things that I've experienced, occurred). My attempt here is to provide a <u>roadmap as a pictorial of my experiences</u>.**

Timeline-

1. Held captive-me laying across the bed stoic as if I couldn't move.

2. Transported-under the cover of a helm that was hovering right above.

3. Picked up the vibes of alien life form present in the closet and was communicating.

4. Reminds me of that song four and twenty black birds...because I've seen too many crows to fathom.

5.In Germany, there was one lone black bird (crow) that was the largest I've ever seen- in the snow. Also, held captive in a room and locked in via shutters.

6. Image of a fan turned into skeleton with a scythe- aka grim reaper.

7. Held captive-sitting up in the bed hearing high pitch voices

An unimaginative person would have dismissed these a long time ago. I couldn't. Being an Experiencer will put you right in the mix. And you won't just be able to dismiss what has happened based on being scared.

Or maybe afraid of the consequences of having known. My very own Pictionary is a way to connect the dots. It shows the patterns (if there are any) as a reminder to me that these events really did take place. I often wonder if some type of schematic could emerge. There's a, what if? aspect to each episode. What if... I couldn't remember (we talked about memory loss in last chapter)? What if...I couldn't engage stealthily, as if being present wasn't enough? (we all can have out of body experiences; but making any associations as to their connections could be hard to do). The last, what if...has to do with the longevity and brevity of the connections that I could make. Would they be due to time, spatial, and/or sequential matters?

My drawings are set as a reminder that I was present and conscious (as in fully awake). These were not necessarily the dreams, but they could have started as such. I also believe that the schematics (drawings) should be true to life, so I will mention a state, country or a city when necessary.

Connecting the dots in this time span as well as timeframes would also coincide with my books. There's a book whereby, I have written about each episode. They represent books one through eight. So, if you are wondering why I am using a roadmap to connect the dots, maybe, as you have experiences that span such a rich timeline, you might be excited about seeing what pattern could emerge too. The previous eight books written by me, are all very detailed about each event and what took place. The scariest thing to me was wondering what to do with it- after all was said and done. Should I try to see if there's some type of map? A roadmap perhaps as an in road or layout for connecting events.

Was I Safe? *I knew that I had to know.* But somehow, I leaned on the side of caution anyway out of respect for the Beings, as Entities that were contacting me.

No longer resisting this chain of development...I knew that if I *didn't answer the door*-they'd keep knocking.

And...it was OK if I heard it too. So everything *wasn't* strange.

Was I ever safe? If I was, I didn't really know it. It felt that way at different levels, but I leaned toward the side of caution, just in case.

One thing I was scared about (and this was a deep- felt angst too-because never, could my fears be aired out loud) was what caused me to shake sometimes, were the unknowns. What if I wasn't supposed to tell? What if...no one else was ever supposed to see it? And...what if, after all, is said and done, I wouldn't get the 'respect' of having been receptive, while at the same time protecting and respecting the Source. The source of all of this information- seemingly, was ominous.

Here are some definitions pertaining to the Roadmap:

Captive- held down physically and kept in high suspense (with angst) as to what was going to happen

Abducted- as in, taken-taken away from the place I was supposed to be in without really going anywhere

Ominous- knowing about the strangeness-some threatening, some auspicious

Capricious- using undercover and underhanded behavior so as not to reveal it.

Refined behavior- there was now, acceptance.

There was <u>capricious</u> behavior that was being presented to me in a strange fashion.

I had awareness about everything the entire time.

What's capricious about it, was the suspense. The suspense of not knowing 'why' I was being taken or abducted.

I never witnessed unpleasant scenery or was taken to 'visit' a precarious site. With the exception of my dreams; where I knew anything could happen- I'd come to know that I was being 'held down' for a reason.

The reason was simple. It was to get my attention.

When someone or something is holding you captive-against your will; and you are fighting with all, of your power- just to move...that becomes <u>ominous</u>. And you can no longer express that feeling of being safe.

But that feeling-as a sensation-can get suppressed eventually, as you are prodded to go on.

That's how I felt. I no longer wonder what the knocks mean now. And the ringing of the doorbell.

It's was to get my attention.

So maybe I've passed my fears. And (after coming off, of safe base), I no longer should have to worry about it.

That is absolutely, another level! Another level of achievement of which I am aware.

I didn't want to ask them to stop coming. But I did want the ominous behavior to slow down so that I could at least know when they were coming for me and that it wasn't meant to do me harm. I did feel that way at times- mostly because of the captivity.

The abduction wasn't so bad. In fact, I could get a notion as to what they were doing. It was like a close up and personal encounter with another being-especially the one with the 'floating lady'. In that situation, someone had obviously been taken, like me, but in a different capacity. They were being transported and moving towards something. I was there standing still and erect. The difference between the two of us was that- I was still alive. Frozen in observation-but alive. So, I was supposed to see it.

I know have a bit of refined behavior after having those experiences as opposed to feeling so much angst about it before. Coming from each episode; I've gained more perspective. My view now, is to be more relaxed.

I view them now as recurring events -meaning, they might not ever stop. But I have stopped something I feel maybe is just the scary part. Lessons learned and experience gained. And insight that's turned into perspective.

Maybe the ones (celestial beings) that could do the scary things that could make you fearful -maybe now...they should now have to knock. And it would require your own willingness- to participate. That is a graduation.

I used to want to say, "Don't do this...don't contact me! This is too much! I'm not strong enough for this! But maybe I was. I was receiving Divine Inspiration. That was the counterbalance to anything that I felt was ominous. It came later of course, and I had to go through the things necessary (as a process) to get me there. So, it became-worth it. And I haven't- to this day...shut any doors. The physical doors, maybe. Yes. I did actually at times, jump up to shut my closet door. I had had an experience with what was shown as a figure that was in there. A closet is just a closet after all, and after some thought about it my now refined behavior doesn't let it bother me so much. But, I do from time to time, get up and close the door. Only out of respect for what took place.

If a Being was talking to you (out of the closet), would you accept that as normal or ominous? That rhetorical question was kept in the back of my mind and it became a habit for me to shut the door. Me shutting the door was a sign of not feeling safe. It also let me know that ALL contact wouldn't necessarily be good contact if it kept lingering even though you knew it was gone. And that wasn't the only contact I'd had. I had experienced several others. Others that rose to the level of me being just plain fearful.

There was another reason for not feeling safe, at times, as well. It is what I call, the 'shake up'.

The shakeup is when I could be writing something down with a pen or typing on the computer-that's when my pen would act as if it was 'stuck'. Or I could go through a whole paragraph and then be hit with 'scribble'. It was as if my instrument suddenly didn't want to move or wanted to strike something out that didn't need to be there. That's when I knew that there was more to it and that the spirits of divinity were guiding me. Ominous, as in the pen striking 12 (on a clock) - figuratively. In one of my other books, I mentioned how the spirit can capture you similar- to the way that people can find themselves speaking in tongues in a religious or spiritual setting. For me, when writing, it was like I was 'missing the mark' or had 'gone off track'. That's when I knew I wasn't supposed to say it. It got struck out-literally- and I erased it. Or more or less dispensed with it because with wasn't a word or phrase that was supposed to be used.

That's when I learned that words mean something. And that's why I have also included a dictionary for many of the words I try to explain. The dictionary helps put it to use in a big way. So, I have gotten use to- Divine Wisdom striking- even with the stoke of a pen. I also knew that I wasn't supposed to back track- and remain scared.

The half- baked little girl that used to run away (when she felt that something was wrong and there was nothing she could do about it) had developed into a 'tough' lady who had been blessed to be present in the Eyes of the Lord. So yes, I do count my blessings. Especially when its coming from the spirit. I have always felt -helped- in some way. But now, I knew it.

Divinity prods us to get things done, but we can't always do it our own way. We should have to be guided- so that we can learn our lessons.

An Act of God

Based on my very own Roadmap, that I am showing you that has a pattern, I have talked about the neospams that I have mentioned earlier in my previous books as to what they should mean to us. The steps of abduction and captivity were between a host of events. All of it was for me to learn how to be able to walk in my own shoes and to learn also that I should share the light. Any blessings gathered from all of it was that God was showing me that there was more to what I thought exists and that sometimes being taken is the only way of being shown. And regardless of 'how' I might have thought of the act as being ominous or capricious, that my fear of reprisal – the one that held tightly and tucked away beneath the chest- was done so as to bring my attention to what was most important. Showing me the way back to and how to get to God. So, it is a road- one that I was taken on and had participated in for the purpose of me being able to write my ninth book- which was my opening to what I now call- refined behavior. I've earned the maturity of it, not via my age- but through a series of progressions.

Knowing about the things that could be Everlasting, Is like striking Gold. It is understanding that the Master has a Masterplan. It was an act of

God to get me out of my angst and release me to the 'field of lillies' where I could forever feel free and play as a little girl. With me, I carry a spirit. And it all pertains to my roadmap. Knowing that there aren't ever any new changes or breaches in the synergies- that there is just code switching that's being done all the time. Here is a picture of my Roadmap (*reference last pages in book of picture titled Roadmap).

My Quote: *"Never think that we can ever fall short (or let go) of our truest desire; when our truest desire, is to learn about self"* -IJ

10 GRADUATIONS

As seen through the eyes of an Experiencer; I've seen things through Graduations. And I am now at the graduation- of what I consider to be *Retrospect*

My first two books were the foundation.

"When Crows Call" and "Crows 2: Rings of Truth-The Afterthought".

Hook, line, and sinker; there's no way someone could read those two and say- 'I've never experienced something like that.' Quite the contrary, they're both, relatable. To be honest, out of body experiences (at least telling about them) can be pretty, scary. Kind of like when I was listening to my granddaughter's friends 'take on his story and version of events as to why he was meditating in complete darkness. I found something a bit scary with his story, but not because of the actual practice of meditating, which I see no problems with, but because of something that he said. If you reference anything strange -as to your experiences, whether you put them in a book or not, people can always find something that's at least a little scary about them, if not strange. This habit is something that we all have and are prone too. And I truly, believe, that is why God has chosen a series of graduations as steps to prevent us from shutting down before we can be fully processed. Imagine the overload, of learning something all at once. I mentioned this earlier. We could be taken off balance if something out of the ordinary wasn't due to us learning it via our own experience. That's why we can take exceptions to a story, unless it's our own version. Experiencers will tell about what they have gone through. And it will be as an iteration- which is their version (of the tale).

My third book came about as if someone was speaking directly to me and holding my hand while I was writing the words. It was called "The Most Controversial Book in the Entire Universe"-it was written at my third iteration or generation of a book. Whatever the (previsions) and premonitions, I was having at the time were based on what I went through regarding my previous experiences. It was a profound and in-depth, look, into a medium of exchange in which knowledge was definitely presented to me as if coming from my previous (books) foundations. It was almost like giving me answers. Answers to questions I never sought, I guess, but were meant to be exchanged. I accepted it as such. And thus, my third book was born. If you read that one, you can know more about how my visions were born.

The fourth, fifth and sixth books, I kind of merged them together in understanding. With each, Divine wisdom had struck. I was on a road to redemption it seemed because everything was coming fast as lightening but still only piecemeal. Once I had gained perspective on what it was, I couldn't let it go as a chain of events. Struck like a lightening bulb being screwed out if its socket, I now knew what it was to be frightened. It was a heavy weight to carry a heavy load. One that had me venture into unchartered waters. The territory I was now dispensed with telling about or sharing-had become more surreal. And I was inspired to write them, nonetheless. The books were called: "The Magic of Everything" and, the-Transformative Beliefs series starting with Transformative Beliefs: Intuition and Transformative Beliefs: CounterBalance. Those were the three that pertained to my fourth, fifth and sixth iterations of growth and development in a spiritual sense and with sequential graduations.

At some levels I even said that I was safe. Although venturing into unchartered territory as far as what I was to know- about anything, I didn't take whatever I was 'given' lightly. Divinity has a way of protecting you. I simply felt safe- after writing those books. There was more clarity, and an abundance of knowledge that was gleaning from my perspective. Most of which- I was being passed through-as a medium. I'm not afraid to say this now, but I was before writing those books. So safe base meant a lot to me. It meant that I no longer had to be scared. I didn't fear the writings, or the dictation (divine dictation can be better known as divine interference). Because everything was pertaining to what I had just written previously, it was being formulated as if it were something new. I knew it was my experiences that dictated it-the format. I knew that I wasn't or hadn't been a writer- before -all of this. What I didn't know, is that it was all parts of a plan. A plan to get me to the next level of the writings of my books. So that I could be prepared for whatever was coming.

One thing I did know is that it was at the sixth book (level), that I felt 'perfectly' safe.

The angst was gone. The queries about the medium of understanding, "why me?'. All, of those thoughts were dissipating, and I had come to accept my fate.

Safe, meant safe, as in -on safe base. And that anything that would be coming after probably would again, make me feel insecure.

I never lost my perspective, however, while gaining the gleaning into my episodes. Somehow, I knew that because everything was coming from divine wisdom, thoughts being transferred, etc. that there was a feeling and spirit of anointing -that was all about how and why, I felt safe.

I felt safe by the time of and throughout the transition of my course of writing my sixth book but didn't know that anything pertaining to it would come after. That's how divine wisdom works. It strikes, you receive it. You translate (the best you can) as part of dictation. And then you just...go with the flow, knowing that you might have added something to the world. It's a safe feeling. However, later on, playing it safe, I realized, wasn't what I was supposed to do.

I had spared giving both names and dates, as part of my writings quest because it all was done is as in a chain of a succession of events. The clarity of which I couldn't reach conclusions until they came through as my visions. What I had written was more profound and it seemed to become more about the visions- that I was to come to know. But people were involved too. Almost, in every situation.

I have now reached the plateau or juncture at which brings me retrospect. Retrospect that's no longer gleaning through smoke and mirrors but is reflecting what's been given to me as straight-with no chasers. I'd have to accept whatever came to past as ominous but also virtuous as well simply because of the arrangement of the signals. I could be writing something that's profound, like with my seventh and eighth book. But all the steps that were taken were pushing me forward to write my ninth.

In this ninth book, are the steps that have taken me closer. Closer to anything than I've ever reached at previous stages. It is where everything has opened up. It is where I have opened up to and become more relaxed. At safe base I felt safe- but I wasn't relaxed. The difference is knowing that you can make a difference as opposed to just writing to get things off your chest. Even though a tenth book might be forthcoming...I am now at my ninth. Which is a visual retrospect - containing a Roadmap, of me, no longer having to play "catch up" with my thoughts. It means that the roadmap was not only real, but true. And it's coming from my first and stemming through my last production of books. Although I consider them as my iterations, most of them had been coming through (initially) as my dreams. It ended up being as a step ladder whereby I needed to climb. And all I could do now was 'show' and not necessarily, to 'tell'.

At this step ladder (stage), I seem to be climbing, and I'm eager to tell, but also show- more. The pictorials presented in this ninth book can be taken as a Roadmap. And the pictures that were drawn and formulated (in my other books), were also parts of my journey. *(see books one through eight)

This ninth book is the one I was chosen for; to bare all, to tell everything. And it definitely, has taken me off of 'safe base'.

Everything that has been shown was in a sequential graduation and occurred at various stages of when I had gone through something.

Some Experiencers don't get to live to tell all-all the time. Unless...they are being blessed to capture it through the divine lens.

It is easy to make an assessment to 'not believe'. And I will share this quote from my nine year old granddaughter, who asked me to say it, if and when I publish my book: "It's up to you, if you can believe it or not."

Nine iterations of truth were represented in my writings. And this is my ninth book.

Nine iterations of growth cycles of which I was unaware of until, I had, actually- completed them.

These weren't 'new' stages. They were there all along, and I was beginning to recognize them as separate, but complete experiences. - I guess I had to wait…at least…until I had completed most of my visions, to put them all together. Which is what occurred at the ninth (book).

Growth cycles that are presented, most likely are us taking steps towards our very own graduations. Heights of which, can be unknown, until we've actually reached them and have become thorough in our understanding (through some sort of experience) to be able to recognize them. Graduations are formations of life's developments taking shape and form and helping us gaining our perspectives. Free flowing- as in thoughts arriving at their destination. Those are the patterns. But 'freestanding' is what we also can be. Which is to formulate our own opinions based on the patterns we've been shown.

Iteration

An iteration won't jump out at you. It is what takes us through our life's growth patterns and cycles. They are the very steps needed to launch from any foundation- that's been set.

For us, to be taken through various episodes that we can experience in our lives-theses stages represent a repass. Formations are the embodiment of who and what we are as we develop but iterations (as a chosen form of repass) takes time. Time that represents stages of growth. We are taken through loops (in computer language) as if passing. When we have reached a bypass, for example, we can be re-interjected or readied for the next stages. It takes a period, of time for these passages; especially if you don't even know what you're passing through. It really doesn't matter how high we reach as far as growth. Sometimes, there is always a place where we can especially remain safe. I can count nine iterations. Books one...two...three...four...five...six...seven...eight...and this one!

For some it could be as growth at any level. Because of a repass (like monopoly having to pass Go all the time with the Exchange of going through our In's and Out's...levels one and two will likely be the beginning stages before you can see a pattern or even recognize the others. The repass gets us where we need to be and it is Divinity that downloads the information.

Equation

I wrote about an existing equation before. An equation exists, for the sake of Life's foundation. The equation represents everything. Everything that is within our sphere, aura, grasp, and reach. It is also what's considered outside.

The equation mostly represents our In's and Out's, as we're switching gears.

In's and Out's, our spirit developing into a person. And in this book, I can also use human being since we are closely connected to divinity.

There is more to life-than what life has created. There's more to put forward about our understanding of life than we should really ever even want to know. It's that simple. That's the equations part. To let us know that our bodies won't always be aware of the equation itself. For us, however, it does represent a life cycle.

One that's attached to the foundation. If you want to know more about the equation as I had explained it in my last book, read, "Transformative Beliefs: The Ultimate Perception". It was my eighth book.

My foundation was to rise higher and higher to achieve a plateau. Which ultimately was presented, as elevation. Every elevation level that I reached- was a plane. I coasted at some. Had wavered and was confused at others. But through Divine Intervention and clairvoyance, my landing became proper and timely and ultimately is what guided me through my experiences.

It took me nine elevations as graduations to experience writing my nine books. Each was written separately and over the course of years. Not only did I NOT plan for this, but the embodiment of my spirit kept rising pushing me to help recount and retell those past experiences that were exceptional and had become my stories- as seen through a divine lens.

They have become the embodiment of my very own truths. I never sought to be, act, or think 'higher'. Just as I never have sought out anything as pertaining to what was beyond or behind the light- what I sought were 'my truths'. And those ended up as episodes that took me off my safe base. But whatever it is that will comprise the next chapter- in my life. I feel that I am ready for it.

Ending

"For every moment that I get awakened-by such things as 'the knocks at the door, or 'the doorbell rings'...even if I discover that no one is there...I will know that it is being done by something spiritual, that's contacting me in a physical way."

~The Ultimate visions have created the Ultimate Book-which is "Hatching the Ideal Belief's" ~

*this section has-<u>Divinely Inspired Back pages and pictorial diagrams of the Centrifuge as represented in the book:</u>

Earthlinks centrifuge-earth has linkages to our bodies: the cause and effect gives us this exchange.

The outer sphere reverts, back in and the core turns as directional.

Everything comes to the core-its built like a fan, but the core is hollow, meaning-there is nothing.

Something that can stir it can be a body or shell which requires a seed to be planted. Then, the core does what it's supposed to do.

Deep in the shells core we have reverberation when there is movement or something to stir it. Our inner spirit seeks to come out (as in gone), while the outside is like tempered glass and becomes a shield that holds (together) the whole thing.

The center is divided into sections as if coming from the core. The core has centrifuge in it (inert gases are what ignite the fuse). *we become gases when we escape* it is the gases that create the stir-then rotation and reaction as reverberation to exchange life for every soul.

*At the center of the core is its directional flow which rebounds into something called earth.

What is the pivot that's at the center of the hole that pulls its centrifuge down to be ignited?

There's a pivotal point by design (that's precise) in which the core gets its direction. It's made in the matter of a split second and that's how we get the 'flash'. The flash is the centrifuge serving as ignition whereby everything gets to rotate.

Shells fuel the core -the more that can be planted, the better.

We think that we live on the surface. But it is because of everything that's planted, that we can continue to grow. So, earth, as a compound, was made so that everything could be 'planted'. This happens over and over. If we are ever to leave this earth -we lose our weight-and become lifted because we lose our bodies that were designed to be filled. The correlation is like what can be lifted because of the center of balance. Our effigy (as a bodies figure and form) is to model the synergies "code switching" as it happens above ground. It is Divinity -Linkage into our spirit.

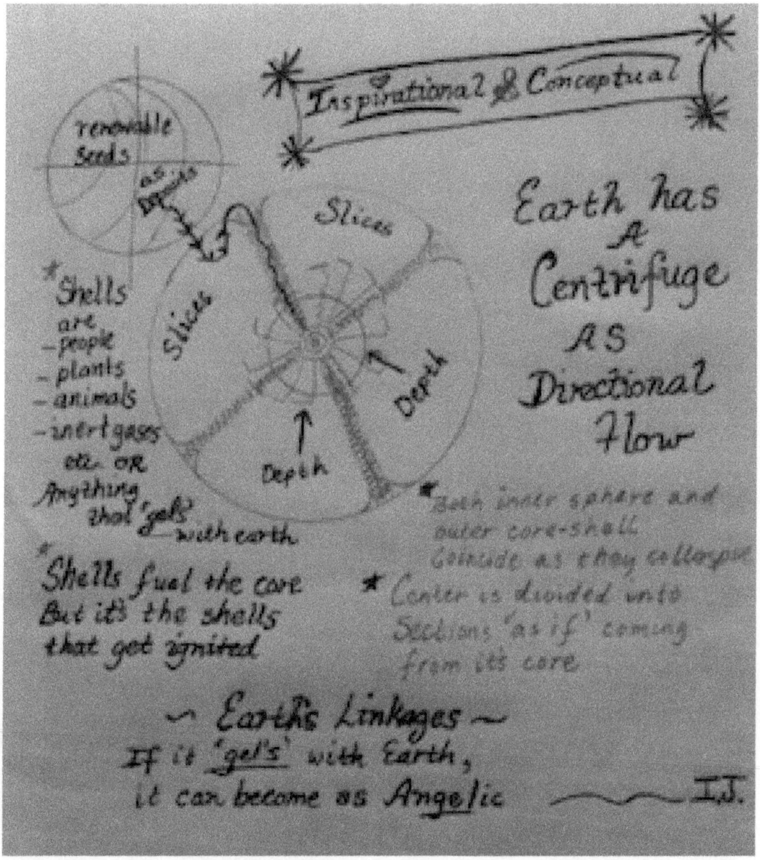
Inspirational & Conceptual
renewable Seeds
Slices
Slices
Depth
Depth
Earth has A Centrifuge AS Directional Flow
*Shells are
- people
- plants
- animals
- inert gases
etc. OR
Anything that 'gels' with earth
*Shells fuel the core
But it's the shells that get ignited
*Both inner sphere and outer core-shell Coincide as they collapse
* Center is divided into Sections 'as if' coming from it's core
~ Earth's Linkages ~
If it 'gel's' with Earth,
it can become as Angelic
I.J.

Back pages continued...

These Things Happened:

The Connecting of the dots of my roadmap is:

a topography as related (in pictures) to the places, and spaces, of where and when I was at the time...those events happened. Coordination of events are in sequences and span of years that were also mentioned in my previous books. This roadmap provides an overview.

~No matter how we tie in technology, Spiritually, it can't get more TECHNIFIC than that!

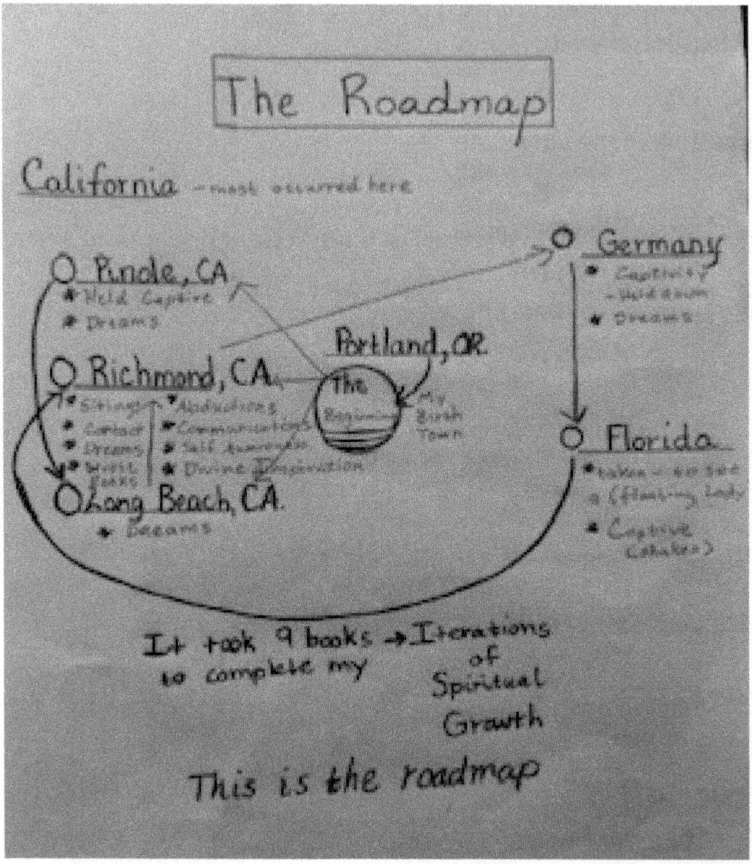
The Roadmap
California
Pinole, CA
* Held Captive
* Dreams
Richmond, CA
Portland, OR
The
My
Birth
Town
Long Beach, CA
* Dreams
Germany
* Dreams
Florida
It took 9 books → Iterations of Spiritual Growth
to complete my
This is the roadmap

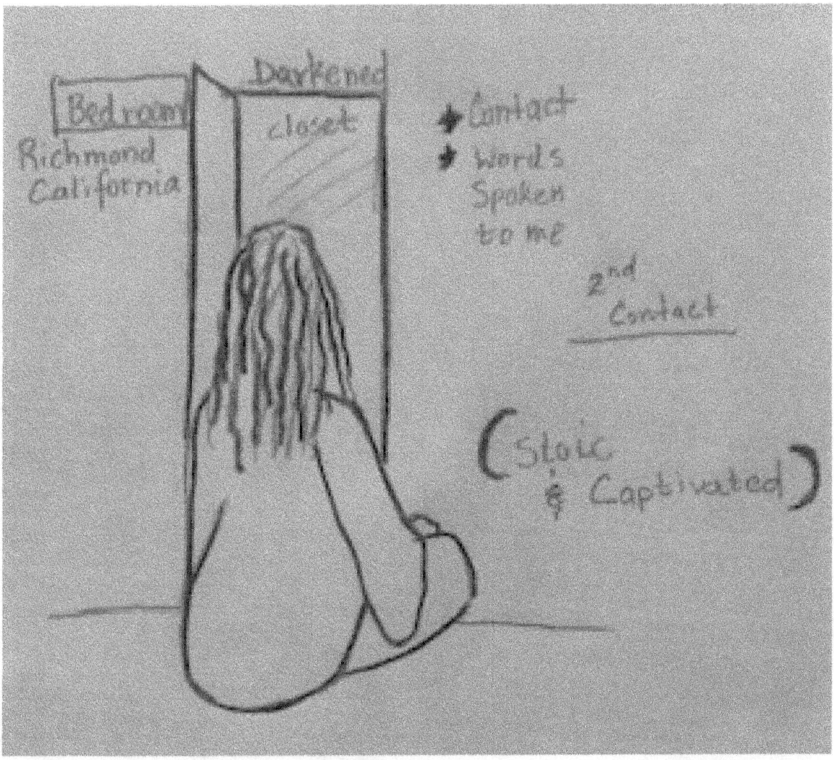
Bedroom
Richmond
California
Darkened
closet
Contact
words
Spoken
to me
2nd
Contact
(Stoic
& Captivated)

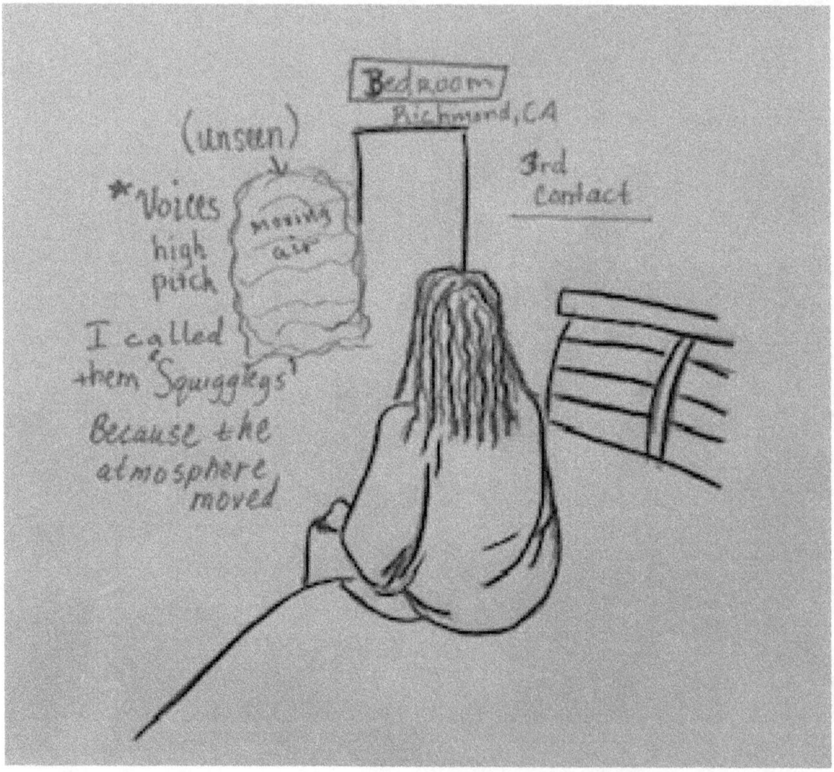
Bedroom
Richmond, CA
(unseen)
3rd
Contact
moving
air
*Voices
high
pitch
I called
them 'Squigglegs'
Because the
atmosphere
moved

ABOUT THE AUTHOR

While born and raised in Portland, Oregon, I moved to California for the scenic view of the beaches. Spending half time between southern and northern California initially, I finally settled on making the Bay Area my home. I have traveled abroad to Italy, Germany, and other countries. And have visited and or lived in several places throughout the United States. I have two Master's degrees: one in Cyber security, the other in Professional Studies. **Fun Facts about me:**

*I have eight siblings- (many of whom are still living). I am very, close (in relations) to all, of my siblings.

*My parents were married at a young age and were together their entire adult lives. Although they are both deceased- I was very, close to my parents and miss them dearly.

*I always knew I was born to do something different. I felt it on the inside and starting at an early age.

* Links in a chain is what I call -my family.